Simple
HEALTHY
MEALS

BREAKFAST TO DESSERT

THE AUSTRALIAN
Women's Weekly

CONTENTS

We've developed a book full of recipes, from breakfast through to dinner, which are easy to prepare, good for the waistline and, best of all, delicious. Dining solo, catering for a crowd or needing to feed starving kids, these recipes will soon become a source of vital inspiration in your kitchen – no hard-to-find ingredients, no slaving over the stove; like the title suggests, just simple healthy meals.

Pamela Clark

Food Director

minted tomato, rhubarb and lime frappe

preparation time 15 minutes cooking time 10 minutes makes 1¼ litres (5 cups)

4 cups coarsely chopped rhubarb (440g)

¼ cup (55g) sugar

¼ cup (60ml) water

4 medium tomatoes (600g), peeled, seeded, chopped coarsely

2½ tablespoons lime juice

3 cups ice cubes

2 tablespoons coarsely chopped fresh mint

1 Combine rhubarb, sugar and the water in medium saucepan; simmer, covered, about 10 minutes or until rhubarb is tender. Cool.

2 Blend or process rhubarb mixture with remaining ingredients until smooth.
PER 250ML *0.4g fat; 334kJ (80 cal)*

DRINKS

papaya, strawberry and orange juice

preparation time 5 minutes **makes** 1 litre (4 cups)

1 large papaya (1.2kg), chopped coarsely
250g strawberries
¾ cup (180ml) orange juice

1   Blend or process ingredients until smooth.
    TIPS Refrigerate ingredients before making the juice. Serve the
    juice within 30 minutes of making.
    PER 250ML *0.3g fat; 368kJ (88 cal)*

orange, carrot and ginger juice

preparation time 5 minutes **makes** 1 cup (250ml)

1 large orange (300g), peeled, chopped coarsely
1 small carrot (70g), halved lengthways
2cm piece fresh ginger (10g)

1   Push orange, carrot and ginger through juice extractor into glass.
    TIPS Refrigerate ingredients before making the juice. Serve the
    juice within 30 minutes of making.
    PER 250ML *0.3g fat; 439kJ (105 cal)*

banana passionfruit soy smoothie

preparation time 5 minutes **makes** 1 litre (4 cups)

You need about six passionfruit for this recipe.

½ cup (125ml) passionfruit pulp
2 cups (500ml) soy milk
2 medium ripe bananas (400g), chopped coarsely

1   Strain passionfruit pulp through sieve into small bowl; reserve liquid and seeds.
2   Blend or process passionfruit liquid, milk and banana until smooth. Stir in reserved seeds.
     PER 250ML *4.7g fat; 656kJ (157 cal)*

mixed berry smoothie

preparation time 5 minutes **makes** 1 litre (4 cups)

250ml frozen low-fat strawberry yogurt, softened slightly
1⅓ cups (200g) frozen mixed berries
3 cups (750ml) skim milk

1   Blend or process ingredients until smooth.
     PER 250ML *1.7g fat; 782kJ (187 cal)*

pineapple orange frappe

preparation time 5 minutes **makes** 1 litre (4 cups)

1 medium pineapple (1.25kg), chopped coarsely
½ cup (125ml) orange juice
3 cups ice cubes
1 tablespoon finely grated orange rind

1   Blend or process ingredients until smooth.
    PER 250ML *0.2g fat (0g saturated); 309kJ (74 cal)*

coconut mango thickshake

preparation time 10 minutes (plus freezing time) **serves** 6

3 medium mangoes (1.3kg)
¾ cup (180ml) coconut milk
1½ cups (375ml) milk
2 cups (500ml) vanilla ice-cream

1   Remove skin from mangoes; chop flesh coarsely. Freeze flesh
    about 2 hours or until firm.
2   Blend or process frozen mango with milks and ice-cream
    until smooth.
    TIP For a reduced-fat version of the thickshake, substitute light
    coconut milk, skim milk and low-fat ice-cream. You can also use
    peaches, nectarines, plums, apricots, bananas or berries, or a
    combination if you prefer, instead of the mango.
    PER SERVING *13.9g fat; 1145kJ (274 cal)*

sweet saffron lassi

preparation time 5 minutes makes 3 cups (750ml)

Lassis are yogurt-based drinks which are an excellent cooling foil for a fiery Indian curry.

pinch saffron threads

1 tablespoon boiling water

2 cups (560g) yogurt

1 cup (250ml) iced water

2 tablespoons caster sugar

½ teaspoon ground cardamom

1 cup ice cubes

1   Combine saffron and the boiling water in small heatproof cup; stand 5 minutes.
2   Whisk yogurt, the iced water, sugar and cardamom in large jug; stir in saffron mixture and ice cubes.
    PER 250ML 6.4g fat; 782kJ (187 cal)

spiced iced coffee milkshake

preparation time 10 minutes (plus standing and cooling time) makes 1 litre (4 cups)

¼ cup (20g) coarsely ground coffee beans

¾ cup (180ml) boiling water

2 cardamom pods, bruised

¼ teaspoon ground cinnamon

1 tablespoon brown sugar

1½ cups (375ml) low-fat vanilla ice-cream

2½ cups (625ml) skim milk

1   Place coffee then the water in coffee plunger; stand 2 minutes before plunging. Pour coffee into small heatproof bowl with cardamom, cinnamon and sugar; stir to dissolve sugar. Cool 10 minutes.
2   Strain coffee mixture through fine sieve into blender or processor; blend or process with ice-cream and milk until smooth.
    PER 250ML 3g fat; 640kJ (153 cal)

iced mocha

preparation time 5 minutes serves 2

1 tablespoon instant coffee granules

1 tablespoon boiling water

2 tablespoons chocolate-flavoured topping

1½ cups (375ml) milk

2 cups (500ml) vanilla ice-cream

½ cup (125ml) thickened cream, whipped

1 teaspoon drinking chocolate powder

1 Combine coffee and the water in medium heatproof jug; stir until dissolved. Stir in chocolate-flavoured topping and milk.

2 Pour chocolate milk into two large glasses; top each with ice-cream and cream. Sprinkle with sifted drinking chocolate.
PER SERVING 43.9g fat; 2696kJ (645 cal)

spiced chocolate milk

preparation time 10 minutes serves 2

30g dark eating chocolate, melted

2 cups (500ml) milk

1 cinnamon stick

1 Using a teaspoon, drizzle melted chocolate onto the insides of heatproof glasses.

2 Combine milk and cinnamon stick in medium saucepan; stir over low heat until heated through, but not boiling. Remove cinnamon. Pour milk into heatproof serving glasses.
PER SERVING 14.1g fat; 1020kJ (244 cal)

DRINKS

10

vanilla cafe latte

preparation time 5 minutes serves 2

⅓ cup (30g) coarsely ground coffee beans

2 cups (500ml) milk

1 teaspoon vanilla extract

1 Combine ingredients in medium saucepan; stir over low heat
   until heated through, but not boiling.
2 Strain coffee mixture through fine sieve into heatproof serving
   glasses.
   PER SERVING *9.9g fat; 765kJ (183 cal)*

real hot chocolate

preparation time 10 minutes serves 2

---

1 litre (4 cups) milk

200g milk eating chocolate, chopped coarsely

100g dark eating chocolate, chopped coarsely

¾ cup (180ml) thickened cream

1 tablespoon coffee-flavoured liqueur

90g choc-coated crispy malt balls, chopped coarsely

1 Combine milk and chocolates in medium saucepan; stir over low
   heat until chocolate is melted.
2 Meanwhile, beat cream and liqueur in small bowl with electric
   mixer until soft peaks form.
3 Divide chocolate milk between heatproof serving glasses; top
   with cream mixture, sprinkle with malt balls.
   PER SERVING *35.3g fat; 2328kJ (557 cal)*

citrus compote

preparation time 20 minutes (plus standing time) serves 4

2 large limes (160g)

3 large oranges (900g)

2 medium pink grapefruit (850g)

2 teaspoons sugar

½ vanilla bean, split

1 tablespoon small fresh mint leaves

1 Grate the rind of 1 lime and 1 orange finely; reserve grated rind. Peel remaining lime, remaining oranges, and grapefruit.

2 Segment all citrus over a large bowl, reserving juice. Combine segments in large bowl with sugar, vanilla bean, reserved rind and reserved juice. Stand, covered, 5 minutes; sprinkle with mint leaves.

TIP Pink or ruby grapefruit have coral-pink flesh and a shell-pink blush to their skin, and are sweeter than the yellow-skinned variety

PER SERVING 0.7g fat; 685kJ (164 cal)

BREAKFAST

ROLLED BARLEY

ROLLED RICE

ROLLED RYE

ROLLED TRITICALE

ROLLED OATS

porridge with rolled grains

We used water to make these porridges, but skim milk or various fruit juices are an option, if you like. The amounts given below for each type of porridge are enough to make 4 servings

GRAIN	AMOUNT	SOAKING LIQUID	COOKING LIQUID	COOKING TIME	MAKES
ROLLED RICE	¾ cup (75g)	1½ cups (375ml)	¾ cup (180ml)	10 minutes	1¾ cups *per serving 238kJ (57 cal);* *0.5g fat (0g saturated fat);* *0.6g fibre; 14.8g carbohydrate*
ROLLED BARLEY	¾ cup (75g)	1½ cups (375ml)	¾ cup (180ml)	25 minutes	1½ cups *per serving 276kJ (66 cal);* *0.1g fat (0.1g saturated fat);* *2.1g fibre; 11.5g carbohydrate*
ROLLED OATS	¾ cup (60g)	1½ cups (375ml)	½ cup (125ml)	10 minutes	½ cups *per serving 233kJ (56 cal);* *1.3g fat (0.2g saturated fat);* *1g fibre; 9.3g carbohydrate*
ROLLED RYE	¾ cup (75g)	1½ cups (375ml)	1½ cups (375ml)	50 minutes	1¾ cups *per serving 248kJ (59 cal);* *0.5g fat (0.2g saturated fat);* *2.3g fibre; 12.1g carbohydrate*
ROLLED TRITICALE	¾ cup (75g)	1½ cups (375ml)	1½ cups (375ml)	45 minutes	1¼ cups *per serving 244kJ (58 cal);* *0.5g fat (0g saturated fat);* *0.3g fibre; 11.7g carbohydrate*

1 Place grain and soaking liquid in medium bowl, cover; stand at room temperature overnight.
2 Place undrained grain in medium saucepan; cook, stirring, until mixture comes to a boil. Add cooking liquid, reduce heat; simmer, uncovered, for required cooking time. Serve warm with toppings of your choice

toppings

These toppings are enough for a single serving of porridge.

½ cup (125ml) skim milk	0.1g fat; 189kJ (45 cal)
1 teaspoon honey	0g fat; 94kJ (23 cal)
1 tablespoon low-fat vanilla yogurt	0g fat; 68kJ (16 cal)
pinch cinnamon	0g fat; 6kJ (2 cal)
½ mashed small banana (65g)	0.1g fat; 240kJ (57 cal)
1 tablespoon dried fruit	0.1g fat; 156kJ (37 cal)
2 teaspoons toasted shredded coconut	2g fat; 79kJ (19 cal)

toasted muesli

preparation time 15 minutes cooking time 45 minutes (plus cooling time) serves 2

1 cup (90g) rolled oats

¼ cup (15g) unprocessed bran

¼ cup (35g) finely chopped dried apricot

¼ cup (20g) finely chopped dried apple

2 tablespoons sultanas

1 tablespoon honey

1 tablespoon water

1 cup (250ml) skim milk

1 Preheat oven to 150°C/130°C fan-forced.

2 Combine oats, bran and fruit in medium bowl; stir in combined honey and water.

3 Spread mixture onto oven tray; bake, uncovered, about 45 minutes or until toasted, stirring occasionally. Cool.

4 Serve muesli with milk, and fresh fruit, if you like.

PER SERVING *4.4g fat; 1433kJ (343 cal)*

STORE Muesli can be refrigerated in an airtight container for up to 1 month.

blueberry muffins

preparation time 10 minutes cooking time 20 minutes makes 12

cooking-oil spray

1 cup (150g) self-raising flour

1 cup (160g) wholemeal self-raising flour

½ cup (100g) firmly packed brown sugar

1 cup (150g) fresh or frozen blueberries

2 egg whites, beaten lightly

⅓ cup (80ml) prepared apple sauce

¾ cup (180ml) skim milk

1 Preheat oven to 200°C/180°C fan-forced.

2 Lightly spray 12-hole (⅓-cup/80ml) muffin pan with oil.

3 Sift flours into large bowl; stir in sugar and berries.

4 Stir in egg white, sauce and milk until almost combined (do not over-mix); divide batter among pan holes.

5 Bake about 20 minutes.

PER MUFFIN *0.5g fat; 545kJ (130 cal)*

STORE Muffins can be made a day ahead and kept in an airtight container at room temperature. Suitable to freeze up to 3 months.

BREAKFAST

16

strawberry hotcakes with blueberry sauce

preparation time 15 minutes **cooking time** 20 minutes **serves** 4

1 egg, separated

2 egg whites

½ cup (125ml) prepared apple sauce

½ teaspoon vanilla extract

2 cups (560g) low-fat natural yogurt

1¾ cups (280g) wholemeal self-raising flour

250g strawberries, chopped coarsely

BLUEBERRY SAUCE

1 cup (150g) blueberries, chopped coarsely

2 tablespoons sugar

1 tablespoon water

1 Beat egg whites in small bowl with electric mixer until soft peaks form.
2 Combine egg yolk, sauce, extract, yogurt, flour and strawberries in large bowl; fold in egg whites.
3 Make blueberry sauce.
4 Pour ¼-cup batter into heated lightly greased large frying pan. Cook about 2 minutes or until bubbles appear on the surface. Turn hotcake; cook until lightly browned on other side. Remove from pan; cover to keep warm. Repeat with remaining batter. Serve hotcakes drizzled with blueberry sauce.

BLUEBERRY SAUCE Combine ingredients in small saucepan; bring to a boil, stirring constantly. Reduce heat; simmer, uncovered, 2 minutes. Remove from heat; cool. Blend or process cooled mixture until smooth.

PER SERVING *3.4g fat; 1639kJ (391 cal)*

roast garlic mushrooms with crispy ham

preparation time 10 minutes cooking time 25 minutes serves 2

200g button mushrooms

150g flat mushrooms, halved

100g swiss brown mushrooms

1 medium red onion (170g), sliced thinly

1 clove garlic, crushed

1 tablespoon lemon juice

coarsely ground black pepper

cooking-oil spray

8 basil leaves, torn

200g shaved light leg ham

½ small french bread (75g), sliced thickly

1   Preheat oven to 200°C/180°C fan-forced.
2   Combine mushrooms, onion, garlic, juice and pepper in shallow medium baking dish; spray lightly with oil. Cook, uncovered, about 20 minutes or until mushrooms are tender. Stir in basil.
3   Meanwhile, spread ham on oven tray; cook, uncovered, about 15 minutes or until crisp.
4   Toast bread both sides. Serve bread topped with ham, then mushroom mixture.
    PER SERVING *5.2g fat; 1103kJ (264 cal)*
    STORE *Cook recipe just before serving.*

mini spinach frittata

preparation time 10 minutes cooking time 20 minutes serves 2

250g baby spinach leaves

½ teaspoon olive oil

1 small brown onion (80g), sliced thinly

1 tablespoon water

pinch ground nutmeg

2 egg whites, beaten lightly

2 tablespoons skim milk

½ teaspoon olive oil, extra

1   Steam or microwave spinach until tender. Drain; chop roughly.
2   Heat oil in medium saucepan; add onion and the water. Cover; cook, stirring occasionally, until onion is soft. Combine spinach, onion mixture, nutmeg, egg white and milk in medium bowl.
3   Lightly grease four egg rings with a little of the extra oil; heat remaining extra oil in large frying pan. Place egg rings in pan; divide egg mixture among rings.
4   Cook until mixture is set; remove egg rings. Turn frittata; cook frittata until lightly browned underneath. Serve with a green salad, if you like
    PER SERVING *0.8g fat; 194kJ (46 cal)*

corned beef hash patties with poached eggs

preparation time 10 minutes cooking time 15 minutes serves 2

1 medium brown onion (150g),
chopped finely

3 medium potatoes (600g), grated coarsely

500g cooked corned beef, shredded finely

2 tablespoons finely chopped
fresh flat-leaf parsley

2 tablespoons plain flour

2 eggs, beaten lightly

1 tablespoon vegetable oil

4 eggs, extra

1 tablespoon finely shredded fresh basil

1 Combine onion, potato, beef, parsley, flour and egg in large bowl. Using hand, shape mixture into four patties.
2 Heat oil in large frying pan; cook patties until browned both sides and cooked through.
3 Break extra eggs into greased egg rings in barely simmering water; poach eggs until cooked as desired. Carefully lift rings away from eggs; lift eggs from water with slotted spoon, drain.
4 Serve hash patties topped with poached eggs; sprinkle with basil.
   PER SERVING *37.8g fat; 3387kJ (810 cal)*

maple rice pudding with pecans and dates

preparation time 10 minutes cooking time 40 minutes serves 8

1½ litres (6 cups) milk

2 cups (500ml) cream

⅔ cup (160ml) maple syrup

¼ teaspoon ground cinnamon

⅔ cup (130g) white medium-grain rice

½ cup (85g) coarsely chopped dried dates

½ cup (70g) roasted pecans,
chopped coarsely

1 Combine milk, cream, syrup and cinnamon in large saucepan; bring to a boil, stirring occasionally. Reduce heat; stir in rice. Cook, uncovered, over low heat, stirring occasionally, about 40 minutes or until rice is tender.

2 Serve rice pudding with combined dates and nuts; drizzle with a little more maple syrup, if you like.
   PER SERVING *41.1g fat; 2420 kJ (579 cal)*

bacon, cheese and chilli muffins

preparation time 10 minutes cooking time 30 minutes makes 18

8 rindless bacon rashers (520g),
 chopped coarsely

2½ cups (375g) self-raising flour

80g butter, chopped coarsely

1 teaspoon sweet paprika

½ teaspoon dried chilli flakes

1½ cups (180g) coarsely grated
cheddar cheese

310g can corn kernels, drained

1 egg

1 cup (250ml) buttermilk

1 Preheat oven to 200°C/180°C fan-forced. Oil three 6-hole (⅓-cup/80ml) muffin pans.

2 Cook bacon in heated medium frying pan, stirring, until crisp; drain on absorbent paper.

3 Process flour, butter, paprika and chilli until mixture resembles breadcrumbs. Transfer to medium bowl; stir in bacon, cheese, corn and combined egg and buttermilk.

4 Divide mixture between pan holes; bake about 20 minutes or until cooked when tested. Turn muffins onto wire rack; serve warm.
   PER MUFFIN *10.2g fat; 836kJ (cal 200)*
   TIP These muffins are best made using a strong vintage cheddar.

Plum tomatoes, also known as roma or egg tomatoes, are small and oval in shape; they are often used in Italian dishes.

breakfast with the lot

preparation time 10 minutes cooking time 25 minutes serves 4

2 large plum tomatoes (180g), quartered

4 eggs

4 slices multigrain bread (180g)

60g light ham

50g baby spinach leaves

1 Preheat oven to 200°C/180°C fan-forced. Line oven tray with greaseproof paper.

2 Place tomato, cut-side up, on tray; roast, uncovered, about 25 minutes or until softened and lightly browned.

3 Meanwhile, place enough water in a large shallow non-stick frying pan to come halfway up the side; bring to a boil. Break eggs, one at a time, into small bowl, sliding each into pan; allow water to return to a boil. Cover pan, turn off heat; stand about 4 minutes or until a light film of egg white has set over each yolk.

4 Toast bread until lightly browned both sides.

5 Using an egg slide, remove eggs, one at a time, from pan; place egg, still on slide, on absorbent-paper-lined saucer to blot up any poaching liquid. Serve toast topped with ham, spinach, egg, then tomato.

PER SERVING *7g fat; 680kJ (160 cal)*

chocolate hazelnut croissants

preparation time 15 minutes cooking time 15 minutes makes 8

2 sheets ready-rolled puff pastry

⅓ cup (110g) chocolate-hazelnut spread

30g dark eating chocolate, grated finely

25g butter, melted

1 tablespoon icing sugar mixture

1 Preheat oven to 200°C/180°C fan-forced. Lightly grease two oven trays.

2 Cut pastry sheets diagonally to make four triangles. Spread chocolate over triangles, leaving a 1cm border; sprinkle each evenly with grated chocolate.

3 Roll triangles, starting at one wide end; place 3cm apart on trays with the tips tucked under and the ends slightly curved in to form crescent shape. Brush croissants with melted butter.

4 Bake, uncovered, about 12 minutes or until croissants are browned lightly and cooked through. Dust croissants with sifted icing sugar.
   PER CROISSANT *17.7g fat; 1153kJ (275 cal)*

SNACKS

toast of the town

Raise your glass in a toast to crusty, delectable bruschetta (pronounced broos-ketta). What could be easier than bread topped with the following flavour combinations? And the praise for these little numbers will be overwhelming.

bruschetta with three toppings

preparation time 5 minutes cooking time 5 minutes makes 25

All toppings are enough for one bread stick .

1 small french bread (150g)
2 cloves garlic, peeled, halved
2 tablespoons olive oil

1   Trim ends from bread stick, cut bread into 1cm-thick slices. Grill bread both sides until browned lightly. Rub garlic over one side of each piece of toast; brush with oil. Top with desired topping.

courgette and pine nut

preparation time 10 minutes cooking time 10 minutes makes 25

2 tablespoons olive oil
1 tablespoon pine nuts
1 clove garlic, crushed
1 baby aubergine (60g), chopped finely
1 small tomato (130g), chopped finely
2 small courgettes (180g), chopped finely
6 seeded black olives, chopped finely
2 tablespoons sultanas
2 teaspoons red wine vinegar
1 tablespoon finely chopped fresh basil
1 tablespoon finely chopped fresh flat-leaf parsley

1   Heat oil in medium frying pan; cook nuts, garlic and eggplant, stirring, 5 minutes. Add tomato, courgette, olives, sultanas and vinegar; cook, stirring, until courgette is soft. Cool. Stir in herbs. Divide vegetable mixture among toasts.
PER SERVING *4.2g fat; 421kJ (100 cal)*

roasted red pepper & olive

preparation time 5 minutes cooking time 10 minutes **makes** 25

2 large red peppers (700g)

1 tablespoon lemon juice

2 teaspoons drained capers

1 clove garlic, crushed

¼ cup finely chopped fresh flat-leaf parsley

1 teaspoon ground cumin

2 teaspoons sugar

⅓ cup (40g) seeded black olives, sliced thinly

1 Quarter peppers, discard seeds and membranes. Roast, uncovered, under grill, skin-side up, about 5 minutes or until skin blisters and blackens. Cover pepper pieces in plastic or paper for 5 minutes; peel away skin.

2 Blend or process pepper with juice, capers, garlic, parsley, cumin and sugar until smooth; stir in olives. Divide pepper mixture among toasts.
  PER SERVING *2.4g fat; 360kJ (86 cal)*

tomato and basil

preparation time 5 minutes **makes** 25

3 small tomatoes (270g), seeded, chopped finely

1 small red onion (100g), chopped finely

¼ cup finely shredded fresh basil

1 tablespoon olive oil

1 Combine ingredients in small bowl. Divide tomato mixture among toasts. Top with small fresh basil leaves, if you like.
  PER SERVING *2.4g fat; 167kJ (40 cal)*

dips

Avoid the temptation to snack on junk food high in saturated fat by keeping a supply of bagel chips and healthy dips on hand. Serve them to guests too – they'll never know they're eating low-fat!

bagel chips

preparation time 10 minutes **cooking time** 15 minutes (plus cooling time) **serves** 4

4 bagels

3 teaspoons vegetable oil

2 cloves garlic, crushed

½ teaspoon dried oregano leaves

1   Preheat oven to 150°C/130°C fan-forced.
2   Using a sharp knife, cut bagels into very thin slices. Place slices in single layer on oven trays; lightly brush one side of each slice with combined oil, garlic and oregano.
3   Bake, uncovered, about 15 minutes or until lightly browned; cool chips on trays.
    PER SERVING *5.3g fat; 1481kJ (354 cal)*
    STORE Chips can be stored in an airtight container for 1 month.

baba ghanoush

preparation time 10 minutes (plus refrigeration time) **cooking time** 35 minutes (plus cooling time) **serves** 4

2 small eggplants (460g)

⅓ cup (95g) low-fat natural yogurt

1 tablespoon lemon juice

2 cloves garlic, crushed

1 teaspoon tahini

1 teaspoon ground cumin

½ teaspoon sesame oil

2 tablespoons finely chopped fresh coriander leaves

1   Preheat oven to 200°C/180°C fan-forced.
2   Halve eggplant lengthways; place on oven tray. Bake, uncovered, about 35 minutes or until tender. Cool; remove and discard skin.
3   Blend or process eggplant with remaining ingredients until smooth. Cover; refrigerate about 30 minutes.
    PER SERVING *2.2g fat; 218kJ (52 cal)*

spicy tomato salsa

preparation time 10 minutes **cooking time** 15 minutes (plus cooling time) **serves** 4

4 medium tomatoes (600g), chopped finely

2 cloves garlic, crushed

1 small brown onion (80g), sliced thinly

1 teaspoon cajun seasoning

2 teaspoons tomato paste

1   Combine ingredients in small saucepan. Cook, stirring, about 15 minutes or until onion is soft and sauce has thickened; cool.
    PER SERVING *0.4g fat; 153kJ (37 cal)*
    STORE Salsa can be made up to 3 days in advance and refrigerated, covered.

quick beetroot dip

preparation time 10 minutes **serves** 4

225g can sliced beetroot, drained well

¼ cup (70g) low-fat natural yogurt

1 teaspoon ground coriander

2 teaspoons ground cumin

1   Blend or process all ingredients until smooth.
    PER SERVING *0.6g fat; 137kJ (33 cal)*
    STORE Dip can be made up to 3 days in advance and refrigerated, covered.

From top to bottom spicy tomato salsa, baba ghanoush, quick beetroot dip.

caramelised onion and red lentil dip

preparation time 10 minutes cooking time 15 minutes makes 2½ cups

¾ cup (150g) red lentils

2 cups (500ml) water

2 cloves garlic, quartered

1 medium potato (200g), chopped coarsely

¼ cup (60ml) olive oil

2 medium brown onions (300g), sliced thinly

½ teaspoon ground cumin

1 teaspoon ground coriander

¼ teaspoon sweet paprika

2 tablespoons lemon juice

1 Combine lentils, the water, garlic and potato in medium saucepan; bring to a boil. Reduce heat; simmer, uncovered, about 15 minutes or until lentils soften, stirring occasionally.

2 Meanwhile, heat 2 tablespoons of the oil in medium frying pan; cook onion, stirring occasionally, about 10 minutes or until caramelised. Remove 2 tablespoons of the onion from pan; reserve. Add spices to pan; cook, stirring, until fragrant. Remove from heat; stir in juice.

3 Blend or process lentil mixture and onion with remaining oil until dip is smooth. Top with reserved onion; serve with toasted turkish bread or pitta crisps, if you like.

PER TABLESPOON *2g fat; 153kJ (37 cal)*

chilli pizza rounds

preparation time 10 minutes cooking time 10 minutes makes 12

2 tablespoons finely chopped fresh oregano

⅓ cup (80g) low-fat ricotta cheese

1 fresh small red thai chilli, seeded, chopped finely

1 tablespoon tomato paste

6 slices wholemeal bread (270g)

2 tablespoons finely grated parmesan cheese

1 Combine oregano, cheese, chilli and paste in medium bowl.

2 Cut two 5cm-rounds from each slice of bread; grill rounds until lightly browned on both sides.

3 Spread rounds with cheese mixture; sprinkle with parmesan. Grill about 5 minutes or until cheeseis melted. Sprinkle with extra oregano leaves, if you like.

PER PIZZA *1.7g fat; 277kJ (66 cal)*

vegetarian pizza

preparation time 20 minutes (plus standing time) cooking time 25 minutes serves 2

7g sachet (2 teaspoons) dried yeast

½ teaspoon sugar

½ cup (125ml) warm water

1½ cups (225g) plain flour

1 teaspoon vegetable oil

¼ cup (65g) tomato paste

½ cup (100g) canned drained red kidney beans

1 small red onion (100g), sliced thinly

1 small courgette (90g), sliced thinly

1 small red pepper (150g), sliced thinly

4 baby mushrooms (40g), sliced thinly

¼ cup (25g) coarsely grated light mozzarella cheese

1 tablespoon finely grated parmesan cheese

1 tablespoon fresh basil leaves

1 Combine yeast and sugar in large bowl; stir in the water. Cover; stand in warm place about 10 minutes or until mixture is frothy.

2 Sift flour into another large bowl; stir in yeast mixture and oil. Mix to a firm dough.

3 Turn dough onto lightly floured surface; knead about 5 minutes or until dough is smooth and elastic.

4 Return dough to bowl; cover. Stand in warm place about 45 minutes or until doubled in size. Turn dough onto lightly floured surface; knead until smooth.

5 Preheat oven to 200°C/180°C fan-forced.

6 Roll dough large enough to line 20cm pizza tray. Spread dough with paste; top with remaining ingredients, except basil. Bake, uncovered, about 25 minutes or until crust is crisp. Remove from oven; sprinkle with basil.

PER SERVING *7.9g fat; 2427kJ (581 cal)*

STORE Uncooked pizza can be prepared up to 3 hours in advance and refrigerated, covered.

MAINS

vegetable moussaka

preparation time 10 minutes cooking time 50 minutes (plus cooling time) serves 2

1 large aubergine (500g), sliced thickly

2 large tomatoes (440g), chopped finely

1 teaspoon sugar

2 teaspoons margarine

1 tablespoon plain flour

1 cup (250ml) skim milk

2 tablespoons finely grated parmesan cheese

2 tablespoons finely chopped fresh basil

1 Preheat oven to 200°C/180°C fan-forced.

2 Place aubergine, in single layer, on oven tray; bake, uncovered, 15 minutes. Turn, bake 15 minutes or until browned lightly; cool 10 minutes.

3 Combine tomato and sugar in small saucepan; cook, stirring occasionally, about 30 minutes or until tomato is soft and liquid almost evaporated.

4 Meanwhile, melt margarine in another small saucepan; add flour. Cook; stirring, 1 minute. Gradually add milk; stir over medium heat until sauce boils and thickens. Stir in half the cheese and half the basil. Stir remaining basil through tomato mixture.

5 Divide one-third of tomato mixture, aubergine and cheese sauce between two 2-cup (500ml) ovenproof dishes; repeat with two more layers. Sprinkle with remaining cheese.

6 Bake, uncovered, about 15 minutes or until moussaka is lightly browned.

PER SERVING *6.1g fat; 867kJ (207 cal)*

STORE Moussaka can be prepared up to 3 hours in advance and refrigerated, covered.

roasted vegetable lasagne

preparation time 40 minutes (plus standing time) cooking time 1 hour serves 6

3 medium red peppers (600g)

2 medium aubergines (600g), sliced thinly

2 tablespoons coarse cooking salt

2 medium courgettes (240g), sliced thinly

600g kumara, sliced thinly

cooking-oil spray

700g bottled tomato pasta sauce

4 fresh lasagne sheets

⅔ cup (160g) ricotta cheese, crumbled

1 tablespoon finely grated parmesan cheese

WHITE SAUCE

40g low-fat dairy-free spread

¼ cup (35g) plain flour

1½ cups (375ml) skim milk

2 tablespoons coarsely grated parmesan cheese

1 Preheat oven to 240°C/220°C fan-forced.

2 Quarter peppers; discard seeds and membranes. Roast, uncovered, skin-side up, about 5 minutes or until skin blisters and blackens. Cover pepper pieces in plastic or paper for 5 minutes; peel away skin.

3 Reduce oven temperature to 200°C/180°C fan-forced. Place aubergine in colander, sprinkle with salt; stand 20 minutes. Rinse aubergine under cold water; pat dry with absorbent paper.

4 Place aubergine, courgette and kumara, in single layer, on oven trays; spray with oil. Roast, uncovered, about 15 minutes or until tender.

5 Meanwhile, make white sauce.

6 Oil deep rectangular 2.5-litre (10-cup) ovenproof dish. Spread 1 cup of the pasta sauce over base of dish; top with half the aubergine and half the pepper. Layer with lasagne sheet; top with ½ cup of the pasta sauce, ricotta, kumara and courgette. Layer with another lasagne sheet; top with remaining pasta sauce, remaining aubergine and remaining pepper. Layer remaining lasagne sheet over vegetables; top with white sauce, sprinkle with parmesan. Bake, uncovered, about 45 minutes or until browned lightly. Stand 5 minutes before serving with rocket salad, if you like.

WHITE SAUCE Melt spread in small saucepan; add flour, cook, stirring, until mixture thickens and bubbles. Remove from heat, gradually stir in milk; cook, stirring, until sauce boils and thickens. Remove from heat; stir in cheese.

PER SERVING 9g fat; 1300kJ (311 cal)

TIP Use scissors to trim lasagne sheets to fit into your baking dish; you may only need three sheets in total.

artichoke risotto

preparation time 10 minutes cooking time 25 minutes serves 6

While the short-grained arborio is traditionally used in a risotto, we chose to use the long-grained doongara rice here because it has both a lower GI rating and is more amenable to being cooked with the liquids added all at once.

2 teaspoons olive oil

1 medium brown onion (150g), chopped finely

3 cloves garlic, crushed

6 green onions, sliced thinly

2 cups (400g) doongara rice

¾ cup (180ml) dry white wine

1½ cups (375ml) chicken stock

3 cups (750ml) water

400g canned artichoke hearts, drained, sliced thinly

½ cup (40g) finely grated parmesan cheese

1   Heat oil in large saucepan; cook brown onion, garlic and half of the green onion, stirring, until brown onion is soft. Add rice, wine, stock and the water; bring to a boil. Reduce heat; simmer, covered, 15 minutes, stirring occasionally.

2   Stir in artichoke, cheese and remaining green onion; cook, stirring, about 5 minutes or until heated through.

PER SERVING *4.5g fat; 1353kJ (323 cal)*

SERVING SUGGESTION A salad of grape tomatoes, sliced fennel and a few fresh basil leaves suits this risotto perfectly. Continue the Italian theme and serve the risotto with fresh slices of crusty ciabatta, if you like.

vegetable risotto

preparation time 10 minutes (plus standing time) cooking time 45 minutes serves 2

1 small aubergine (230g), chopped finely

1 tablespoon coarse cooking salt

2 teaspoons olive oil

1 small brown onion (80g), chopped finely

1 clove garlic, crushed

¾ cup (150g) brown rice

¾ cup (180ml) chicken stock

2 cups (500ml) water

2 medium courgettes (240g)

2 medium tomatoes (300g),
peeled, chopped finely

125g mushrooms, sliced thinly

¼ cup (20g) coarsely grated parmesan cheese

1 tablespoon fresh oregano leaves

1 Place aubergine in colander; sprinkle with salt. Stand for 30 minutes; rinse well under cold water. Pat dry with absorbent paper.
2 Heat oil in large saucepan; cook onion and garlic until soft. Add rice, stock and the water; bring to boil. Simmer, covered, about 30 minutes or until rice is tender and almost all the liquid is absorbed.
3 Using a vegetable peeler, cut courgette into ribbons.
4 Stir aubergine, courgette, tomato and mushroom into rice; cook, uncovered, about 3 minutes or until vegetables are softened. Stir in half the cheese and oregano; serve risotto sprinkled with remaining cheese.
PER SERVING *11.2g fat; 1923kJ (460 cal)*
STORE Risotto is best made just before serving.

pasta with pesto sauce

preparation time 10 minutes cooking time 10 minutes serves 2

2 cups firmly packed fresh basil leaves

1 clove garlic, crushed

⅓ cup (25g) coarsely grated parmesan cheese

1 tablespoon olive oil

1 tablespoon fat-free french dressing

250g spaghetti

1 Blend or process basil, garlic, cheese, oil and dressing until combined.
2 Cook pasta in large saucepan of boiling water until just tender; drain.
3 Toss pesto through pasta before serving. Sprinkle with extra basil leaves, if you like.
PER SERVING *15.6g fat; 2512kJ (601 cal)*
STORE Pesto can be made up to 3 days in advance and refrigerated, covered.

silverbeet, mushroom and red pepper frittata

preparation time 15 minutes cooking time 45 minutes serves 4

500g silverbeet, trimmed, chopped coarsely

1 tablespoon low-fat dairy-free spread

1 medium brown onion (150g),
chopped finely

2 cloves garlic, crushed

1 medium red pepper (200g),
chopped finely

2 trimmed stalks celery (150g), chopped finely

100g button mushrooms, sliced thinly

2 large carrots (360g), grated coarsely

¼ cup (40g) polenta

¼ cup coarsely chopped fresh basil

3 eggs, beaten lightly

3 egg whites, beaten lightly

⅓ cup (80ml) skim milk

1 Preheat oven to 180°C/160°C fan-forced.

2 Line 20cm x 30cm lamington pan with greaseproof paper.

3 Boil, steam or microwave silverbeet; drain on absorbent paper.

4 Melt spread in deep large frying pan; cook onion and garlic, stirring, until onion is soft. Add pepper, celery and mushroom; cook, stirring, until vegetables just soften.

5 Stir silverbeet, carrot, polenta and basil into vegetable mixture. Remove from heat; cool 5 minutes. Add egg, egg white and milk; stir to combine. Spread frittata mixture into pan; bake, uncovered, about 35 minutes or until lightly browned and firm to touch.

PER SERVING *6.7g fat; 809kJ (193 cal)*

TIP This frittata is just as good eaten at room temperature as it is hot from the oven. Serve frittata with a salad of mixed grape, cherry and teardrop tomatoes, if you like.

MAINS

49

This Italian interpretation of a low-fat vegetable omelette simplifies the cooking process by oven-baking, rather than completing it on the stove-top.

leek, spinach and mushroom frittata

preparation time 15 minutes **cooking time** 40 minutes **serves** 6

1 teaspoon low-fat dairy-free spread

3 cloves garlic, crushed

1 small leek (200g), sliced thinly

400g button mushrooms, sliced thickly

200g baby spinach leaves

2 eggs

6 egg whites

½ cup (125ml) skim milk

⅓ cup (40g) coarsely grated low-fat cheddar cheese

1 Preheat oven to 160°C/140°C fan-forced.

2 Oil deep 23cm-round cake pan; line base with greaseproof paper.

3 Melt dairy-free spread in medium frying pan; cook garlic and leek, stirring, until leek is soft. Add mushroom; cook, stirring, until mushroom is just tender. Add spinach; cook, stirring, until spinach just wilts. Drain.

4 Whisk eggs, egg whites, milk and cheese in large bowl until combined; stir in vegetable mixture.

5 Pour egg mixture into cake pan. Bake, uncovered, about 30 minutes or until just set. Place frittata under hot grill until browned.

PER SERVING *3g fat; 380kJ (91 cal)*

TIP Serve with baby spinach leaves, if you like.

egg-white omelette

preparation time 10 minutes cooking time 15 minutes serves 4

150g light ham

200g button mushrooms, sliced thinly

12 egg whites

¼ cup finely chopped fresh chives

2 medium tomatoes (380g), chopped coarsely

½ cup (45g) coarsely grated low-fat cheddar cheese

1   Trim fat from ham; cut into thin strips. Cook ham in heated large frying pan, stirring, until lightly browned; remove from pan. Cook mushrooms in same pan, stirring, until lightly browned.

2   Beat three of the egg whites in small bowl with electric mixer until soft peaks form; fold in one-quarter of the chives. Pour egg-white mixture into heated lightly oiled 20cm frying pan; cook, uncovered, over low heat until just browned underneath. Place pan under preheated grill; cook until top just sets. Place one-quarter of the tomato on one half of the omelette; return to grill, cook until tomato is hot and top is lightly browned. Gently place a quarter of each of the cheese, ham and mushroom on tomato-half of omelette; fold over to enclose filling. Carefully transfer omelette to serving plate; cover to keep warm.

3   Repeat step 2 with remaining egg whites, chives and fillings.

4   Serve omelttes with toast, if you like.
     PER SERVING *2.4g fat; 707kJ (169 cal)*

MAINS

salmon and herb soufflés

preparation time 10 minutes cooking time 25 minutes serves 2

210g can pink salmon, drained

1 tablespoon finely chopped fresh chives

1 tablespoon finely chopped fresh flat-leaf parsley

pinch cayenne pepper

1 tablespoon margarine

1 tablespoon plain flour

½ cup (125ml) skim milk

2 egg whites

1 Preheat oven to 180°C/160°C fan-forced.

2 Grease two 1-cup (250ml) soufflé dishes . Combine salmon, herbs and pepper in large bowl.

3 Melt margarine in medium saucepan; stir in flour. Cook until bubbling; remove from heat. Gradually stir in milk; stir over heat until sauce boils and thickens. Stir sauce into salmon mixture.

4 Beat egg whites in small bowl with electric mixer until soft peaks form; fold into salmon mixture. Divide mixture between dishes.

5 Bake, uncovered, about 20 minutes or until cooked.
   PER SERVING *14.3g fat; 1075kJ (257 cal)*
   STORE Make recipe just before serving.

beef in red wine

preparation time 15 minutes cooking time 1 hour 15 minutes serves 2

350g beef blade steak

2 medium brown onions (300g), chopped finely

1 clove garlic, crushed

100g mushrooms, sliced thickly

410g can tomato puree

2 teaspoons Worcestershire sauce

½ cup dry red wine (125ml)

1 trimmed stalk celery (100g), chopped coarsely

2 medium carrots (240g), chopped coarsely

2 tablespoons fresh flat-leaf parsley leaves

1 Trim beef; cut beef into 2cm cubes. Cook beef in heated large saucepan until browned. Add onion, garlic and mushroom; cook, stirring, about 2 minutes or until onion is soft. Stir in puree, sauce and wine; bring to a boil. Reduce heat; simmer, covered, about 45 minutes.

2 Add celery and carrot; cook, covered, 15 minutes or until vegetables are tender. Serve sprinkled with parsley, and couscous, if you like.
   PER SERVING *8g fat; 1708kJ (409 cal)*
   STORE Recipe can be made up to a day in advance and refrigerated, covered.

Wasabi is available in both paste and powdered forms. We used the paste but, if you add a few drops of cold water to the powder, as instructed on the label, you can use this mixture as a substitute.

salmon rice paper rolls

preparation time 30 minutes (plus standing time) **serves** 4

50g rice vermicelli

250g asparagus, trimmed

⅓ cup (80g) light sour cream

2 teaspoons finely chopped fresh dill

¼ teaspoon wasabi

2 teaspoons finely grated lemon rind

12 x 22cm-round rice paper sheets

400g smoked salmon

1 small red onion (100g), sliced thinly

60g snow pea sprouts

1 Place vermicelli in medium heatproof bowl, cover with boiling water, stand until just tender; drain.

2 Boil, steam or microwave asparagus until just tender; drain.

3 Combine sour cream, dill, wasabi and rind in small bowl.

4 Place 1 sheet of rice paper in medium bowl of warm water until just softened. Lift from water carefully; place on board.

5 Place 1 slice of salmon on one edge of rice paper. Spread with sour cream mixture, top with 2 asparagus spears, onion, sprouts and vermicelli. Roll up to enclose filling (one end will remain open).

6 Repeat with remaining rice paper rounds and filling.
PER ROLL *4g fat; 452kJ (108 cal)*
STORE Make recipe just before serving.

Baby spinach leaves, along with baby rocket, are the greens of choice for many people today. And why not? They can be used in everything from salads to stir-fries to soups, with no preparation or pre-cooking required; they're full of nutrients; and their respective singular flavours add something special to the dishes in which they are used.

salmon patties with baby spinach

preparation time 30 minutes   **cooking time** 45 minutes   **serves** 4

1kg medium potatoes, chopped coarsely

415g can pink salmon, drained, flaked

6 green onions, chopped finely

2 trimmed stalks celery (200g), grated coarsely

1 teaspoon finely grated lemon rind

⅓ cup (80ml) lemon juice

2 egg whites

2 tablespoons water

2 cups (200g) packaged breadcrumbs

1 teaspoon vegetable oil

230g can water chestnuts, drained, sliced thinly

600g baby spinach leaves

1 tablespoon light soy sauce

¼ cup (60ml) mirin

2 teaspoons sugar

1   Preheat oven to 220°C/200°C fan-forced.

2   Boil, steam or microwave potato until tender; drain. Mash potato in large bowl until smooth; cool slightly. Stir in salmon, onion, celery, rind and half of the juice.

3   Using hand, shape fish mixture into 16 patties. Dip patties, one at a time, in combined egg white and water, then in breadcrumbs. Place patties on lightly oiled oven tray. Cover; refrigerate 30 minutes.

4   Cook patties, uncovered, about 30 minutes or until golden brown and heated through.

5   Meanwhile, heat oil in wok or large frying pan; stir-fry water chestnuts 1 minute. Add spinach, remaining juice, sauce, mirin and sugar; stir-fry until spinach just wilts. Top spinach with salmon patties to serve.

PER SERVING *7.2g fat; 1203kJ (288 cal)*

SERVING SUGGESTION Accompany patties with lemon wedges.

oven-steamed ocean trout

preparation time 10 minutes cooking time 15 minutes serves 4

4 x 200g ocean trout fillets

2 tablespoons lemon juice

1 tablespoon drained capers, chopped coarsely

2 teaspoons coarsely chopped fresh dill

1.2kg large new potatoes, sliced thickly

1 Preheat oven to 200°C/180°C fan-forced.

2 Place each fillet on a square of foil large enough to completely enclose fish; top each fillet with equal amounts of juice, capers and dill. Gather corners of foil squares together above fish, twist to close securely.

3 Place parcels on oven tray; cook about 15 minutes or until fish is cooked as desired. Remove fish from foil before serving.

4 Meanwhile, boil, steam or microwave potato until tender. Serve fish with potato.

PER SERVING *7.9g fat; 1751kJ (418 cal)*

TIP Use tweezers to remove any bones from fish.

SERVING SUGGESTION Accompany trout with mixed salad leaves.

cantonese steamed ginger snapper

preparation time 10 minutes cooking time 30 minutes serves 4

If snapper is unavailable, use your favourite whole firm-fleshed fish for this recipe.

8cm piece fresh ginger (40g)

4 small whole snapper (1.2kg)

¼ cup (60ml) vegetable stock

4 green onions, sliced thinly

½ cup firmly packed fresh coriander leaves

⅓ cup (80ml) light soy sauce

1 teaspoon sesame oil

1 Peel ginger; cut into thin strips lengthways, then cut into matchstick-size pieces.

2 Score fish three times both sides; place each fish on a separate large sheet of foil. Sprinkle with ginger and drizzle with half the stock; fold foil loosely to enclose fish.

3 Place fish in large bamboo steamer; steam fish, covered, over wok of simmering water for about 30 minutes or until cooked through.

4 Transfer fish to serving dish; sprinkle with onion and coriander, then drizzle with combined remaining stock, sauce and oil. Serve with steamed broccoli and baby corn, if you like.

PER SERVING *3.2g fat; 573kJ (137 cal)*

Traditional garlic prawns are given a South-East Asian tweak in this stir-fry. Buk choy has become as common a vegetable staple as green beans or broccoli in most kitchens, and not without good reason. It's versatile, easy to cook and keeps well.

garlic prawns and buk choy with herbed rice

preparation time 20 minutes **cooking time** 15 minutes **serves** 6

1kg medium uncooked prawns

6 cloves garlic, crushed

2 teaspoons finely chopped fresh coriander

3 fresh small red thai chillies, seeded, chopped finely

⅓ cup (80ml) lime juice

1 teaspoon sugar

1 tablespoon peanut oil

1kg baby buk choy, quartered lengthways

6 green onions, sliced thinly

1 tablespoon sweet chilli sauce

HERBED RICE

2 cups (400g) jasmine rice

2 tablespoons coarsely chopped fresh coriander

1 tablespoon coarsely chopped fresh mint

1 tablespoon coarsely chopped fresh flat-leaf parsley

1 teaspoon finely grated lime rind

1 Shell and devein prawns, leaving tails intact.
2 Combine prawns in large bowl with garlic, coriander, chilli, juice and sugar.
3 Heat half of the oil in wok or large frying pan; stir-fry prawns, in batches, until just changed in colour.
4 Heat remaining oil in wok; stir-fry buk choy, onion and sauce, in batches, until just tender. Return prawns to wok; stir-fry until hot. Serve prawns on herbed rice.

HERBED RICE Cook rice, uncovered, in large saucepan of boiling water until tender; drain. Return rice to pan; combine with remaining ingredients.

PER SERVING *4.5g fat; 1602kJ (383 cal)*

chorizo-stuffed roast chicken

preparation time 25 minutes cooking time 1 hour 35 minutes serves 4

20g butter

1 medium brown onion (150g), chopped finely

1 chorizo sausage (170g), diced into 1cm pieces

1½ cups (110g) stale breadcrumbs

½ cup (100g) ricotta cheese

1 egg

¼ cup finely chopped fresh flat-leaf parsley

¼ cup (35g) roasted slivered almonds

1.6kg chicken

2 medium lemons (280g), cut into wedges

SPINACH AND RED ONION SALAD

150g baby spinach leaves

1 small red onion (100g), sliced thinly

1 tablespoon red wine vinegar

2 tablespoons olive oil

1 Melt half the butter in medium frying pan; cook onion and chorizo, stirring, until onion is soft. Cool 10 minutes; combine chorizo mixture in medium bowl with breadcrumbs, cheese, egg, parsley and nuts.

2 Preheat oven to 200°C/180°C fan-forced.

3 Wash chicken under cold water; pat dry inside and out with absorbent paper. Tuck wing tips under chicken. Trim skin around neck; secure neck flap to underside of chicken with skewers.

4 Fill cavity with chorizo mixture, fold over skin to enclose stuffing; secure with toothpicks. Tie legs together with string. Place chicken and lemon in medium baking dish. Rub chicken all over with remaining butter; roast, uncovered, about 1½ hours or until chicken is cooked through, basting occasionally with juices.

5 Meanwhile, make spinach and red onion salad.

6 Serve chicken with stuffing, lemon and salad.
   SPINACH AND RED ONION SALAD Combine ingredientes in large bowl.
   PER SERVING 68.4g fat; 4042kJ (967 cal)

spanish chicken casserole

preparation time 10 minutes cooking time 1 hour 25 minutes serves 4

1 tablespoon olive oil

4 chicken drumsticks (600g)

4 chicken thigh cutlets (800g)

1 large brown onion (200g), chopped finely

4 medium potatoes (800g), quartered

½ cup (80g) roasted pine nuts

½ cup (80g) roasted blanched almonds

3 cups (750ml) chicken stock

1 cup (250ml) dry white wine

⅓ cup (80ml) lemon juice

4 cloves garlic, crushed

2 tablespoons fresh thyme leaves

½ cup coarsely chopped fresh flat-leaf parsley

500g baby green beans, trimmed

1 Preheat oven to 180°C/160°C fan-forced.

2 Heat oil in large flameproof casserole dish; cook chicken, in batches, until browned.

3 Cook onion in same dish, stirring, until soft. Return chicken to dish with potato, nuts, stock, wine, juice, garlic, thyme and half the parsley; bring to a boil. Cover; cook in oven about 1 hour or until chicken is cooked through.

4 Meanwhile, boil, steam or microwave beans until tender; drain.

5 Serve chicken with beans; sprinkle with remaining parsley.

PER SERVING *61.4g fat; 4050kJ (969 cal)*

TIP When using wine in cooking, as a general rule of thumb you should never cook with a wine you wouldn't drink; the wine you use doesn't have to be expensive, but it does have to be drinkable. If you don't want to use white wine, you could substitute water, ginger ale or white grape juice.

chicken and lentil cacciatore

preparation time 15 minutes cooking time 40 minutes serves 4

cooking-oil spray

8 skinless chicken thigh fillets (880g), halved

1 medium brown onion (150g), chopped finely

300g button mushrooms, halved

1 clove garlic, crushed

2 x 410g cans crushed tomatoes

1 tablespoon tomato paste

1 cup (250ml) chicken stock

⅓ cup (65g) red lentils

½ cup (60g) seeded black olives

1 tablespoon drained capers

2 teaspoons finely chopped fresh oregano

2 tablespoons finely chopped fresh flat-leaf parsley

1 Lightly spray large saucepan with oil. Cook chicken until browned, turning occasionally. Remove from pan.

2 Add onion, mushroom and garlic to pan; cook, stirring, until onion is soft. Add undrained tomatoes, paste, stock and lentils.

3 Return chicken to pan; simmer, covered, about 30 minutes or until chicken is cooked. Stir in olives, capers, oregano and parsley.

PER SERVING *17.3g fat; 1858kJ (444 cal)*

STORE Recipe can be made up to a day ahead and refrigerated, covered.

ginger chicken kebabs

preparation time 15 minutes (plus marinating time) cooking time 15 minutes serves 2

300g chicken breast fillets, chopped coarsely

1 tablespoon green ginger wine

1 tablespoon japanese soy sauce

1 tablespoon lemon juice

1 teaspoon vegetable oil

2 teaspoons Worcestershire sauce

2 teaspoons brown sugar

1 teaspoon dijon mustard

1 teaspoon grated fresh ginger

1 Combine ingredients in large bowl; refrigerate, covered, 3 hours or overnight.

2 Thread chicken onto skewers; reserve marinade. Cook kebabs on heated oiled grill plate (or grill or barbecue), brushing frequently with marinade, until chicken is cooked. Serve sprinkled with sliced green onions, if you like.

PER SERVING *10.6g fat; 1091kJ (261 cal)*

STORE Chicken is best marinated a day ahead and refrigerated, covered.

chicken, lemon and artichoke skewers

preparation time 20 minutes cooking time 10 minutes serves 4

3 medium lemons (420g)

2 cloves garlic, crushed

¼ cup (60ml) olive oil

600g chicken breast fillets, chopped coarsely

800g canned artichoke hearts, drained, halved

24 button mushrooms (300g)

1 Squeeze juice from one lemon (you will need two tablespoons of juice). Combine juice, garlic and oil in small screw-top jar; shake well.

2 Cut remaining lemons into 24 wedges. Thread chicken, artichoke, mushrooms and lemon onto 12 skewers; reserve dressing.

3 Cook skewers on heated oiled grill plate (or grill or barbecue), brushing frequently with dressing, until chicken is cooked.

PER SERVING *22.6g fat; 1534kJ (367 cal)*

grilled tandoori chicken

preparation time 10 minutes (plus marinating time) cooking time 15 minutes serves 2

½ cup (140g) low-fat natural yogurt

1 tablespoon lemon juice

½ teaspoon grated fresh ginger

1 clove garlic, crushed

½ teaspoon sugar

½ teaspoon sweet paprika

¼ teaspoon ground cumin

¼ teaspoon ground coriander

¼ teaspoon ground turmeric

pinch chilli powder

400g chicken breast fillets

TOMATO, RED ONION
AND CORIANDER SALSA

1 small tomato (130g), chopped finely

½ small red onion (50g), chopped finely

1 teaspoon sugar

1 tablespoon finely chopped fresh coriander

1 Combine yogurt, juice, ginger, garlic, sugar, paprika and spices in large bowl. Add chicken; turn chicken to coat in marinade. Refrigerate, covered, 3 hours or overnight.

2 Cook chicken on heated oiled grill plate (or grill or barbecue), brushing frequently with marinade, until cooked. Slice chicken thickly.

3 Meanwhile, make tomato, red onion and coriander salsa.

4 Serve chicken topped with salsa, and steamed rice, if you like.

TOMATO, RED ONION AND CORIANDER SALSA Combine ingredients in small bowl.

PER SERVING *12.5g fat; 1457kJ (349 cal)*

STORE Chicken is best marinated a day ahead and refrigerated, covered.

herb-crusted lamb racks with new potatoes and leek

preparation time 25 minutes cooking time 55 minutes (plus standing time) serves 4

4 x 3-cutlet french-trimmed lamb racks (600g)

¼ cup (20g) fresh white breadcrumbs

1 tablespoon finely chopped fresh rosemary

1 tablespoon finely chopped fresh
flat-leaf parsley

2 teaspoons finely chopped fresh thyme

3 cloves garlic, crushed

3 teaspoons bottled coriander pesto

1kg new potatoes, halved lengthways

cooking-oil spray

1 teaspoon sea salt

2 medium leeks (700g), trimmed

2 teaspoons low-fat dairy-free spread

¼ cup (60ml) chicken stock

¼ cup (60ml) dry white wine

1 Preheat oven to 200°C/180°C fan-forced.

2 Trim fat from lamb. Combine breadcrumbs, herbs, garlic and pesto in small bowl. Using hand, press breadcrumb mixture onto lamb racks, cover; refrigerate until required.

3 Place potato in shallow large baking dish; spray with oil, sprinkle with salt. Roast, uncovered, 20 minutes.

4 Place lamb on top of the potato; roast, uncovered, 10 minutes. Reduce oven temperature to 150°C/130°C fan-forced; cook about 20 minutes or until potato is tender and lamb is cooked as desired.

5 Meanwhile, cut leeks into 10cm lengths; slice thinly lengthways. Melt spread in large frying pan; cook leek, stirring, until leek softens. Stir in stock and wine; bring to a boil. Reduce heat; simmer, uncovered, until liquid reduces by half.

6 Stand lamb 5 minutes before cutting racks into cutlets; serve cutlets with potato and leek.

PER SERVING 13.7g fat; 1829kJ (437 cal)

TIP Herbed breadcrumb mixture can be patted onto racks the day before serving. Cover and refrigerate overnight.

SERVING SUGGESTION Serve with a mixed lettuce leaf salad with a lemon vinaigrette.

pepper-grilled lamb fillets with roasted root vegetables

preparation time 30 minutes cooking time 1 hour serves 8

1kg baby beetroots, trimmed

6 small parsnips (360g), quartered

500g new potatoes, halved

400g baby carrots, trimmed

8 baby onions (200g), halved

4 cloves garlic, peeled

¼ cup (60ml) orange juice

¼ cup (90g) honey

1 tablespoon wholegrain mustard

12 lamb fillets (1.2kg)

1½ tablespoons cracked black pepper

1 Preheat oven to 200°C/180°C fan-forced.

2 Boil, steam or microwave unpeeled beetroot until tender; drain. When cool enough to handle, peel beetroot.

3 Combine beetroot in lightly oiled large baking dish with parsnip, potato, carrot, onion and garlic. Pour combined juice, honey and mustard over vegetables; roast, uncovered, stirring occasionally, about 45 minutes or until vegetables are browned and tender.

4 Meanwhile, coat lamb with pepper. Cook lamb on heated oiled grill plate (or grill or barbecue) until cooked as desired. Cover; stand 10 minutes. Slice lamb thickly.

5 Serve vegetables topped with lamb.

PER SERVING *4.8g fat; 1228kJ (294 cal)*

SERVING SUGGESTION Accompany this recipe with bowl of steamed couscous.

TIP All manner of baby vegetables are available at better greengrocers and some supermarkets. You could also serve baby cauliflower, baby turnips and baby pumpkin with the lamb in this recipe.

lamb hot pot with couscous

600g lamb leg chops

1 tablespoon plain flour

2 teaspoons olive oil

1 medium brown onion (150g), cut into thin wedges

1 teaspoon ground cinnamon

1 teaspoon ground turmeric

1 cup (250ml) water

½ cup (125ml) beef stock

½ cup (85g) seeded prunes

2 tablespoons finely chopped fresh coriander

COUSCOUS

1 cup (200g) couscous

1 cup (250ml) boiling water

1 Trim all visible fat from lamb. Cut lamb into cubes; discard bone. Toss meat in flour.

2 Heat oil in large saucepan; cook onion until soft. Add lamb; cook until lamb is browned. Stir in cinnamon and turmeric; cook, stirring, until fragrant.

3 Stir in the water, stock and prunes; bring to a boil. Reduce heat; simmer, covered, about 30 minutes or until lamb is tender.

4 Meanwhile, make couscous.

5 Serve lamb with couscous, sprinkled with coriander.

COUSCOUS Combine couscous with the water in large heatproof bowl, cover; stand about 5 minutes or until water is absorbed, fluffing with fork occasionally.

PER SERVING *20.3g fat; 3648kJ (873 cal)*

STORE *hot pot can be made a day ahead and refrigerated, covered. Couscous is best made close to serving time.*

MAINS

78

*Use the outer leaves of the lettuce for this recipe.
The patties and yogurt mixture can be prepared
several hours ahead.*

lamb patties with beetroot and tzatziki

preparation time 20 minutes cooking time 10 minutes serves 4

500g lamb mince

1 small brown onion (80g), chopped finely

1 medium carrot (120g), grated coarsely

1 egg, beaten lightly

2 tablespoons finely chopped fresh
flat-leaf parsley

1 clove garlic, crushed

1 teaspoon finely grated lemon rind

½ teaspoon dried oregano leaves

½ cup (140g) natural yogurt

1 clove garlic, crushed, extra

1 lebanese cucumber (130g), seeded,
chopped finely

1 tablespoon finely chopped fresh mint

1 large turkish bread (430g)

outer cos lettuce leaves, shredded

400g can whole baby beetroot,
drained, quartered

1 Combine lamb, onion, carrot, egg, parsley, garlic, rind and oregano in
  large bowl. Using hand, shape mixture into 8 patties.
2 Cook patties on heated oiled grill plate (or grill or barbecue), in batches,
  until cooked as desired.
3 Meanwhile, combine yogurt, extra garlic, cucumber and mint in small
  bowl. Cut bread into four even pieces, split each piece in half crossways;
  toast, cut-side up, until browned lightly.
4 Just before serving, sandwich bread with lettuce leaves, patties, tzatziki
  and beetroot.
  PER SERVING *14.9g fat; 1240kJ (71 cal)*

steak diane

preparation time 10 minutes cooking time 15 minutes serves 4

1 tablespoon olive oil

8 thin slices beef fillet steak (800g)

20g butter

3 cloves garlic, crushed

3 green onions, sliced thinly

1 tablespoon brandy

2 tablespoons Worcestershire sauce

300ml cream

1 Heat oil in large frying pan; cook beef, in batches, until cooked as desired. Cover to keep warm.

2 Melt butter in same pan; cook garlic and onion, stirring, until onion is soft. Add brandy and sauce; bring to a boil. Stir in cream, reduce heat; simmer, uncovered, about 3 minutes or until sauces thickens slightly.

3 Divide beef among serving plates; drizzle with sauce.

PER SERVING *51.1g fat; 2755kJ (157 cal)*

SERVING SUGGESTION Goes well with french fries.

beef, red wine and chilli casserole with polenta

preparation time 15 minutes cooking time 1 hour 45 minutes serves 4

2 teaspoons low-fat dairy-free spread

1.5kg lean beef chuck steak, cut into 3cm pieces

2 cloves garlic, crushed

3 fresh small red thai chillies, seeded, sliced thinly

2 teaspoons dijon mustard

1 large brown onion (200g), sliced thickly

2 medium tomatoes (380g), chopped coarsely

410g can tomato puree

¾ cup (180ml) dry red wine

½ cup (125ml) beef stock

1¼ litres (4½ cups) water

1 cup (170g) polenta

¼ cup (20g) finely grated parmesan cheese

2 tablespoons coarsely chopped fresh flat-leaf parsley

1 Melt spread in large saucepan; cook beef, in batches, until browned. Cook garlic, chilli, mustard and onion in same pan, stirring, until onion is soft. Return beef to pan with chopped tomato; cook, stirring, 2 minutes.

2 Add puree, wine, stock and ½ cup of the water to pan; bring to a boil. Reduce heat; simmer, covered, about 1 hour 30 minutes or until beef is tender, stirring occasionally.

3 Meanwhile, bring the remaining litre of water to a boil in medium saucepan. Add polenta; cook, stirring, about 10 minutes or until thickened. Stir in cheese.

4 Add parsley to casserole; serve casserole with polenta.
   PER SERVING *14.3g fat; 2058kJ (492 cal)*
   SERVING SUGGESTION Serve with baby rocket leaves sprinkled with flaked parmesan and a squeeze of lemon juice, if you like..

beef and onion kebabs

preparation time 20 minutes (plus marinating time) cooking time 10 minutes serves 2

350g lean beef rump steak

9 baby onions (225g), halved

HONEY AND LEMON MARINADE

¼ cup (90g) honey

¼ cup (60ml) lemon juice

2 teaspoons grated fresh ginger

2 teaspoons Worcestershire sauce

¼ cup (60ml) tomato sauce

1 tablespoon finely chopped fresh oregano leaves

1 Remove fat from beef; cut beef into 2cm pieces. Thread steak and onion onto 6 skewers.

2 Make honey and lemon marinade.

3 Place kebabs in shallow dish; drizzle with marinade. Refrigerate, covered, 3 hours or overnight.

4 Cook kebabs on heated grill plate (or grill or barbecue), brushing occasionally with marinade, until beef is cooked as desired. Serve with a bitter leaf salad, if you like.
   HONEY AND LEMON MARINADE Combine ingredients in small bowl.
   PER SERVING *8.3g fat; 1794kJ (429 cal)*

meatballs in rosemary paprika sauce

preparation time 15 minutes cooking time 45 minutes serves 2

250g lean beef mince

½ cup (35g) stale breadcrumbs

1 tablespoon finely chopped fresh
flat-leaf parsley

1 tablespoon finely chopped fresh chives

1 egg white

1 teaspoon Worcestershire sauce

1 teaspoon vegetable oil

250g tagliatelle pasta

ROSEMARY PAPRIKA SAUCE

410g can crushed tomatoes

1 cup (250ml) water

2 tablespoons dry red wine

1 medium brown onion (150g),
chopped finely

½ teaspoon Worcestershire sauce

1 teaspoon sweet paprika

3 sprigs rosemary

1 Combine mince, breadcrumbs, parsley, chives, egg white and sauce in large bowl. Using hand, shape mixture into small meatballs.
2 Heat oil in medium saucepan; cook meatballs until cooked through. Drain on absorbent paper.
3 Meanwhile, make rosemary paprika sauce.
4 Cook pasta in large saucepan of boiling water until tender; drain.
5 Add meatballs to sauce; stir until hot. Serve with pasta, and a mixed green leaf salad, if you like.

ROSEMARY PAPRIKA SAUCE Combine undrained tomatoes with remaining ingredients in medium saucepan; bring to boil. Reduce heat; simmer, uncovered, about 20 minutes or until thickened slightly. Discard rosemary.

PER SERVING 14.5g fat; 3685kJ (882 cal)

STORE Recipe can be made a day ahead and refrigerated, covered.

beef and bean tacos

preparation time 15 minutes cooking time 20 minutes serves 2

1 clove garlic, crushed

80g lean beef mince

½ teaspoon chilli powder

¼ teaspoon ground cumin

300g can kidney beans, rinsed, drained

2 tablespoons tomato paste

½ cup (125ml) water

1 medium tomato (150g), chopped coarsely

4 taco shells

¼ small iceberg lettuce, shredded finely

SALSA CRUDA

½ lebanese cucumber (65g), seeded, chopped finely

½ small red onion (50g), chopped finely

1 small tomato (90g), seeded, chopped finely

1 teaspoon mild chilli sauce

1   Preheat oven to 180°C/160°C fan-forced.

2   Make salsa cruda.

3   Cook garlic and beef in heated large frying pan, stirring, until beef is browned. Add chilli, cumin, beans, paste, the water and tomato; cook, covered, over low heat about 15 minutes or until mixture thickens slightly.

4   Meanwhile, place taco shells on oven tray; toast, uncovered, 5 minutes.

5   Just before serving, fill taco shells with beef mixture, lettuce and salsa cruda.
    SALSA CRUDA Combine ingredients in small bowl.
    PER SERVING *9.2g fat; 1308kJ (312 cal)*

red beef curry

preparation time 10 minutes cooking time 20 minutes serves 4

2 tablespoons peanut oil

500g beef rump, cut into 2cm pieces

1 large brown onion (200g), sliced thinly

¼ cup (75g) red curry paste

1 large red pepper (350g), sliced thinly

150g snake beans, cut into 3cm lengths

1⅔ cups (400ml) coconut milk

410g can crushed tomatoes

¼ cup coarsely chopped fresh coriander

1   Heat half the oil in wok or large frying pan; stir-fry beef, in batches, until browned.

2   Heat remaining oil in same wok; stir-fry onion until soft. Add paste; stir-fry until fragrant. Add pepper and beans; stir-fry until vegetables just soften.

3   Return beef to wok with milk, undrained tomatoes and coriander; stir-fry until sauce thickens slightly.
    PER SERVING *41.9g fat; 2390kJ (571 cal)*
    SERVING SUGGESTION Serve with steamed jasmine rice.

satay beef with rice

preparation time 20 minutes cooking time 20 minutes serves 4

1 litre (4 cups) water

1 cup (200g) basmati rice

1 teaspoon peanut oil

500g lean beef topside, sliced thinly

1 large brown onion (200g), sliced thinly

1 clove garlic, crushed

2 teaspoons grated fresh ginger

2 fresh small red thai chillies, seeded,
chopped finely

1 medium red pepper (200g),
chopped coarsely

1 medium green pepper (200g),
chopped coarsely

100g button mushrooms, halved

225g can bamboo shoots, drained

1 teaspoon mild curry powder

2 teaspoons cornflour

½ cup (125ml) chicken stock

¼ cup (65g) light smooth peanut butter

2 tablespoons oyster sauce

1 tablespoon roasted unsalted coarsely
chopped peanuts

1 Bring the water to a boil in large saucepan; stir in rice. Boil, uncovered, about 15 minutes or until rice is just tender. Drain, rinse under hot water; drain rice again, cover to keep warm.

2 Meanwhile, heat oil in wok or large frying pan; stir-fry beef, in batches, until browned.

3 Stir-fry onion and garlic in same heated wok until onion is soft. Add ginger, chilli, peppers, mushroom, bamboo shoots and curry powder; stir-fry until vegetables are just tender.

4 Blend cornflour with stock in small jug; pour into wok, toss to combine with vegetable mixture. Return beef to wok with peanut butter and oyster sauce; bring to a boil, stirring, until sauce thickens slightly. Stir in nuts; serve with rice.

PER SERVING *14g fat; 2387kJ (570 cal)*

crisp beef with baby buk choy and noodles

preparation time 15 minutes cooking time 15 minutes serves 4

2 tablespoons cornflour

½ teaspoon bicarbonate of soda

600g beef rump steak, sliced thinly

⅔ cup (160ml) peanut oil

2 tablespoons sweet chilli sauce

¼ cup (60ml) kecap manis

1 tablespoon light soy sauce

2 teaspoons sesame oil

1 clove garlic, crushed

2 green onions, chopped finely

400g fresh thin egg noodles

200g shiitake mushrooms, quartered

½ small chinese cabbage (400g),
shredded coarsely

300g baby buk choy, sliced thinly lengthways

1 Combine cornflour and soda in large bowl. Add beef; toss to coat, shaking off excess.

2 Heat a third of the peanut oil in wok or large frying pan; stir-fry a third of the beef until crisp. Drain on absorbent paper; cover to keep warm. Repeat with remaining peanut oil and beef.

3 Combine sauces, sesame oil, garlic and onion in small bowl.

4 Place noodles in large heatproof bowl, cover with boiling water, separate with fork; drain.

5 Stir-fry mushroom in same cleaned heated wok about 2 minutes or until just tender. Add cabbage and buk choy; stir-fry 1 minute. Add beef, sauce mixture and noodles; stir-fry until hot.

PER SERVING *47.3g fat; 3605kJ (861 cal)*

You will need to cook about ⅓ cup (65g) white long-grain rice for this recipe.

fish kebabs with chilli sauce

preparation time 15 minutes (plus marinating time) **cooking time** 15 minutes **serves** 2

300g tuna steaks, cut into 3cm pieces

1 tablespoon japanese soy sauce

1 clove garlic, crushed

¼ teaspoon grated fresh ginger

1 medium red pepper (200g), chopped coarsely

1 medium green pepper (200g), chopped coarsely

2 teaspoons vegetable oil

1 cup cooked white long-grain rice

CHILLI SAUCE

1 fresh small red thai chilli, chopped finely

2 cloves garlic, crushed

1 tablespoon finely chopped fresh coriander

1 tablespoon fish sauce

1 tablespoon lime juice

1½ tablespoons brown sugar

1 tablespoon mirin

⅓ cup (80ml) water

1 Combine fish with sauce, garlic and ginger in large bowl; refrigerate, covered, 1 hour.

2 Meanwhile, make chilli sauce.

3 Thread fish and peppers onto 4 skewers. Brush with oil; cook under hot grill until fish is cooked as desired. Serve kebabs with rice; drizzle with chilli sauce.

CHILLI SAUCE Grind chilli, garlic and coriander to a smooth paste; add remaining ingredients. Transfer mixture to small saucepan; stir over low heat until sugar is dissolved and sauce heated through.

PER SERVING *10.8g fat; 1964kJ (470 cal)*

mashed potatoes three ways

Each of these three different mash recipes takes 15 minutes to prepare and about 15 minutes to cook. The key to perfect mash is to work quickly so that the hot potato is mashed and combined with other warmed ingredients then served immediately.

creamed spinach mash

serves 4

1kg desiree potatoes, chopped coarsely
20g butter
1 clove garlic, crushed
125g baby spinach leaves
300ml cream, warmed

1 Boil, steam or microwave potato until tender; drain.
2 Meanwhile, melt butter in large frying pan; cook garlic and spinach, stirring, until spinach is wilted. Blend or process spinach mixture with half the cream until mixture is smooth.
3 Place hot potato in large bowl; mash until smooth, then stir in spinach puree and remaining cream.
   PER SERVING *37.2g fat; 2025kJ (484 cal)*

fetta and black olive mash

serves 4

1kg desiree potatoes, chopped coarsely

2 tablespoons olive oil

⅔ cup (160ml) buttermilk, warmed

200g fetta cheese, chopped finely

1 cup (120g) seeded black olives, sliced thinly

1   Boil, steam or microwave potato until tender; drain.
2   Place hot potato in large bowl; add half the oil, mash until smooth, then stir in milk, cheese and olive. Drizzle with remaining oil.
     PER SERVING *22.1g fat; 1709kJ (408 cal)*

wasabi mash

serves 4

1kg desiree potatoes, chopped coarsely

⅔ cup (160ml) cream, warmed

1 teaspoon wasabi paste

1   Boil, steam or microwave potato until tender; drain.
2   Place hot potato in large bowl; mash until smooth, then stir in remaining ingredients.
     PER SERVING *17.8g fat; 1266kJ (302 cal)*

tiramisu

preparation time 20 minutes (plus refrigeration time) cooking time 25 minutes serves 12

3 eggs

½ cup (110g) caster sugar

¼ cup (40g) wholemeal self-raising flour

¼ cup (35g) self-raising flour

¼ cup (35g) cornflour

1 teaspoon gelatine

1 tablespoon cold water

1½ cups (300g) low-fat ricotta cheese

¼ cup (60ml) skim milk

¼ cup (55g) caster sugar, extra

2 tablespoons instant coffee granulesr

2 tablespoons boiling water

⅓ cup (80ml) skim milk, extra

½ cup (125ml) coffee-flavoured liqueur

10g dark eating chocolate, grated finely

1 Preheat oven to 180°C/160°C fan-forced. Grease 22cm springform tin; line base with greaseproof paper.

2 Beat eggs in small bowl with electric mixer until thick and creamy. Gradually add sugar, beating until sugar dissolves. Fold triple-sifted flours into egg mixture until just combined. Spread into tin.

3 Bake, uncovered, 25 minutes. Turn onto wire rack to cool.

4 Meanwhile, sprinkle gelatine over the cold water in small heatproof jug; place jug in small saucepan of simmering water, stir until gelatine dissolves. Cool 5 minutes.

5 Blend or process cheese, milk and extra sugar until smooth. With motor operating, add gelatine mixture; process until combined.

6 Dissolve coffee in the boiling water in small bowl; stir in extra milk and liqueur.

7 Cut cake in half horizontally. Return one cake half to same springform tin; brush half the coffee mixture over cake; top with half the cheese mixture. Repeat with remaining cake half, coffee mixture and cheese mixture.

8 Refrigerate tiramisu, covered, 3 hours. Sprinkle top with grated chocolate just before serving.
PER SERVING 4.1g fat; 791kJ (189 cal)

DESSERTS

apple bread and butter pudding

preparation time 20 minutes cooking time 1 hour 10 minutes (plus standing time) serves 6

2 medium apples (300g)

2 tablespoons brown sugar

1 tablespoon water

2½ cups (625ml) skim milk

1 vanilla bean, halved lengthways

4 slices thick fruit bread (220g)

3 eggs

½ teaspoon ground cinnamon

¼ teaspoon ground nutmeg

1 Peel, core and quarter apples; cut each quarter into 3mm slices. Dissolve brown sugar in the water in medium frying pan over low heat, add apples; simmer, uncovered, about 5 minutes or until tender, stirring occasionally.

2 Preheat oven to 160°C/140°C fan-forced. Grease deep 1.5-litre (6-cup) ovenproof dish.

3 Combine milk and vanilla bean in medium saucepan; bring to a boil. Remove from heat; stand, covered, 5 minutes. Discard vanilla bean.

4 Meanwhile, cut bread slices into quarters. Arrange bread and apple in alternate layers in dish.

5 Whisk eggs, cinnamon and nutmeg in medium bowl. Gradually whisk hot milk mixture into egg mixture. Pour egg mixture carefully over bread and apple. Place dish in another large baking dish; add enough boiling water to baking dish to come halfway up side of pudding dish.

6 Bake, uncovered, about 1 hour or until set. Serve with ice-cream or cream, if you like.

PER SERVING *3.6g fat; 698kJ (167 cal)*

chocolate ricotta tart

preparation time 15 minutes (plus refrigeration time) **cooking time** 35 minutes **serves** 8

¼ cup (35g) self-raising flour

¼ cup (40g) wholemeal self-raising flour

2 tablespoons caster sugar

2 teaspoons cocoa powder

30g low-fat dairy-free spread

2 teaspoons water

1 egg yolk

RICOTTA FILLING

150g low-fat ricotta cheese

1 egg

1 egg yolk

¼ cup (70g) low-fat natural yogurt

¼ cup (55g) caster sugar

2 teaspoons plain flour

2 tablespoons dark Choc Bits

2 teaspoons coffee-flavoured liqueur

1 Grease 18cm-round loose-based flan tin.

2 Process flours, sugar, sifted cocoa and spread until crumbly; add the water and egg yolk, process until ingredients just cling together. Knead dough gently on lightly floured surface until smooth, cover; refrigerate 30 minutes.

3 Preheat oven to 200°C/180°C fan-forced.

4 Press dough into tin; cover with greaseproof paper large enough to extend 5cm over edge, fill with dried beans or rice. Place tin on oven tray, bake 10 minutes; remove beans and paper. Bake 5 minutes or until pastry is lightly browned; cool.

5 Meanwhile, make ricotta filling.

6 Reduce oven temperature to 180°C/160°C fan-forced. Pour ricotta filling into tin; bake, uncovered, 20 minutes. Cool; refrigerate until firm.
   RICOTTA FILLING Beat cheese, egg, egg yolk, yogurt, sugar and flour in medium bowl with electric mixer until smooth. Stir in chocolate and liqueur.
   PER SERVING *6.5g fat; 706kJ (169 cal)*

chocolate mousse

preparation time 10 minutes (plus refrigeration time) **serves** 8

The word mousse is a French description for froth or foam, a look usually achieved by lots of kilojoule-laden whipped cream. Here, we've used low-fat fromage frais for equally delicious results, but without the excess fat and energy.

1 tablespoon instant coffee granules

1 tablespoon cocoa powder

2 teaspoons hot water

160g dark eating chocolate, melted

3 cups (800g) vanilla-flavoured fromage frais

50g dark eating chocolate, grated finely, extra

1 Dissolve coffee and cocoa in the water in medium bowl. Stir in melted chocolate and fromage frais; beat with electric mixer until mixture is smooth.

2 Divide mixture among eight ½-cup (125ml) serving glasses. Cover; refrigerate overnight.

3 Serve mousse sprinkled with extra chocolate.
   PER SERVING *8g fat; 941kJ (225 cal)*
   SERVING SUGGESTION Serve mousse topped with fresh berries; raspberries team especially well with chocolate.

vanilla bean ice-cream with espresso sauce

preparation time 10 minutes (plus freezing time) **cooking time** 15 minutes (plus standing time) **serves** 4

1 vanilla bean

1 cup (250ml) light evaporated milk

⅓ cup (80ml) light cream

2 egg yolks

½ cup (110g) caster sugar

½ cup (125ml) boiling water

1 tablespoon ground espresso coffee beans

1 Split vanilla bean lengthways; scrape seeds into small saucepan. Add vanilla bean, milk and cream; bring to a boil. Remove pan from heat, cover; stand 20 minutes. Discard vanilla bean.

2 Meanwhile, beat egg yolks and sugar in small bowl with electric mixer until thick and creamy; gradually stir in vanilla milk mixture.

3 Return mixture to same pan; cook, stirring, about 15 minutes or until mixture thickens slightly (do not allow to boil).

4 Strain mixture through fine sieve into 20cm x 30cm lamington pan, cover surface with foil; cool to room temperature. Freeze until almost set.

5 Place ice-cream in large bowl, chop coarsely; beat ice-cream until smooth. Pour into 14cm x 21cm loaf pan, cover; freeze until ice-cream is firm.

6 Just before serving, combine the water and coffee in coffee plunger; stand 2 minutes before plunging. Cool 5 minutes before pouring over ice-cream.
PER SERVING *7g fat; 965kJ (231 cal)*

chocolate brownie

preparation time 15 minutes cooking time 25 minutes makes 16

2 eggs

⅓ cup (75g) firmly packed brown sugar

2 teaspoons instant coffee granules

2 tablespoons cocoa powder

1 tablespoon water

1 tablespoon olive oil

40g low-fat dairy-free spread, melted

¼ cup (40g) wholemeal self-raising flour

¼ cup (45g) dark chocolate Choc Bits

1 teaspoon cocoa powder, extra

2 teaspoons icing sugar mixture

1 Preheat oven to 180°C/160°C fan-forced. Grease deep 19cm-square cake pan; line with greaseproof paper.
2 Beat eggs and sugar in small bowl with electric mixer until thick and creamy. Transfer to medium bowl.
3 Meanwhile, whisk coffee and cocoa with the water and oil in small bowl until smooth; stir in spread. Fold cocoa mixture into egg mixture, then fold in flour and chocolate. Pour mixture into pan.
4 Bake, uncovered, about 25 minutes or until firm to touch. Stand 30 minutes; turn onto wire rack to cook. Serve brownie dusted with sifted combined extra cocoa and icing sugar mixture, and low-fat ice-cream, if you like.
   PER BROWNIE *3.8g fat; 303kJ (73 cal)*

pears poached in cranberry syrup

preparation time 5 minutes (plus standing time) cooking time 45 minutes serves 4

3 cups (750ml) cranberry juice

⅔ cup (160ml) dry white wine

2 cardamom pods, bruised

½ vanilla bean, halved lengthways

4 medium pears (920g)

1 Combine juice, wine, cardamom and vanilla bean in large saucepan. Add peeled pears to pan; bring to a boil. Reduce heat; simmer, covered, about 25 minutes or until tender. Cool pears in syrup.
2 Remove pears from syrup; strain syrup into medium heatproof bowl. Return 2 cups of the strained syrup to same pan (discard remaining syrup); bring to a boil. Boil, uncovered, about 15 minutes or until syrup is reduced by half. Serve pears, hot or cold, with syrup.
   PER SERVING *0.2g fat; 1178kJ (281 cal)*
   TIP Pears can be poached up to a day ahead; reduce the syrup just before serving.

The long refrigeration times required for this cheesecake are a bonus when entertaining. Make it ahead so you're free to devote all your attention to the rest of the menu on the day of the meal.

lime cheesecake

preparation time 30 minutes (plus refrigeration time) cooking time 10 minutes serves 8

80g plain sweet biscuits

40g low-fat dairy-free spread, melted

2 teaspoons gelatine

1 tablespoon water

⅓ cup (80ml) lime juice

⅔ cup (150g) sugar

½ cup (100g) low-fat ricotta cheese

100g packaged low-fat cream cheese

2 teaspoons finely grated lime rind

3 egg whites

1 Grease 18cm springform pan; line base with greaseproof paper.
2 Blend or process biscuits and dairy-free spread until mixture resembles fine breadcrumbs. Using hand, press biscuit mixture evenly over base of pan. Refrigerate until firm.
3 Meanwhile, sprinkle gelatine over the water in small heatproof jug; place jug in small saucepan of simmering water, stir until gelatine dissolves.
4 Combine juice and sugar in small saucepan. Stir over heat, without boiling, until sugar dissolves; bring to a boil. Reduce heat; simmer, uncovered, 1 minute.
5 Beat cheeses and rind in medium bowl with electric mixer until mixture is smooth.
6 Beat egg whites in small bowl with electric mixer until soft peaks form; with motor operating, gradually add hot sugar syrup. Whisk slightly warm gelatine mixture and egg white mixture into cheese mixture; pour mixture into pan. Cover; refrigerate about 2 hours or until set.

PER SERVING *6.7g fat; 773kJ (185 cal)*

SERVING SUGGESTION Pipe whipped light cream on cheesecake and decorate with thin lime wedges just before serving.

black forest parfaits

preparation time 30 minutes (plus refrigeration time) serves 6

2 x 85g packets cherry jelly crystals

6 mini jam rolls (150g), chopped coarsely

¼ cup (60ml) sweet sherry

425g can pitted black cherries, drained

½ cups (375ml) low-fat vanilla custard

3 x 20g low-fat chocolate bars, chopped coarsely

1 Make jelly according to directions on packet; place in large jug. Refrigerate about 1 hour or until jelly is almost set.

2 Meanwhile, combine jam rolls and sherry in small bowl. Reserve half the jam roll mixture; cover until required. Divide remaining half among six 1⅓-cup (330ml) serving glasses.

3 Pour half the jelly mixture over jam roll mixture in glasses; sprinkle with half the cherries. Refrigerate 5 minutes. Continue layering with remaining jam roll mixture, then all of the custard, the remaining jelly and, finally, the remaining cherries. Cover parfaits; refrigerate overnight.

4 Serve parfaits sprinkled with chocolate, and topped with whipped cream, if you like.
PER SERVING 3.2g fat; 1277kJ (306 cal)

melon granita trio

preparation time 45 minutes (plus freezing time) cooking time 10 minutes serves 8

You need a small rockmelon (1.3kg), a small honeydew (1.3kg), and a small watermelon (1.5kg) for this recipe.

3 cups (750ml) water

1½ cups (330g) sugar

800g seeded, peeled, coarsely chopped rockmelon

800g seeded, peeled, coarsely chopped honeydew melon

800g seeded, peeled, coarsely chopped watermelon

1 Combine the water and sugar in medium saucepan, stir over heat, without boiling, until sugar dissolves; bring to a boil. Reduce heat; simmer, uncovered, without stirring, about 2 minutes or until syrup thickens.

2 Blend or process rockmelon until almost smooth; push through sieve into shallow metal cake pan. Combine with a third of the sugar syrup. Repeat process with honeydew and half of the remaining syrup in separate metal cake pan, then with watermelon and remaining syrup in another cake pan.

3 Cover each pan with foil; freeze about 3 hours or until granita mixtures are just set.

4 Keeping granita mixtures separate, scrape into large bowls, then beat each with electric mixer until smooth. Return each to their respective pans, cover with foil; freeze overnight or until each granita sets firmly.

5 Serve granita, layered in alternate scoops, in individual glasses.
SERVING SUGGESTION granitas are delicious on a hot day served with seasonal fruit salad.
PER SERVING 0.6g fat; 979kJ (234 cal)

honey buttermilk ice-cream with fresh fruit salsa

preparation time 30 minutes (plus freezing time) cooking time 15 minutes serves 6 (approximately 2 litres ice-cream)

2 teaspoons gelatine

¼ cup (60ml) water

1½ cups (375ml) low-fat evaporated milk

½ cup (175g) honey

1½ cups (375ml) buttermilk

FRUIT SALSA

1 small pineapple (800g), chopped coarsely

1 large mango (600g), chopped coarsely

3 medium kiwifruit (255g), chopped coarsely

250g strawberries, chopped coarsely

1 Sprinkle gelatine over the water in small heatproof jug, place jug in small pan of simmering water, stir until gelatine dissolves; cool.

2 Meanwhile, place evaporated milk in medium saucepan; bring to a boil. Remove from heat; stir in gelatine mixture and honey. Transfer to medium bowl; cool.

3 Beat buttermilk in small bowl with electric mixer until buttermilk is frothy.

4 Beat evaporated milk mixture in medium bowl with electric mixer until light and frothy. With motor operating, gradually pour in buttermilk; beat until combined.

5 Pour into 2-litre (8-cup) metal pan. Cover with foil; freeze about 3 hours or until just set.

6 Place ice-cream in large bowl, chop coarsely; beat ice-cream with electric mixer until smooth. Pour mixture into pan, cover with foil; freeze until set.

7 Make fruit salsa. Serve ice-cream with fruit salsa.

    FRUIT SALSA Combine ingredients in medium bowl.

    PER SERVING *7g fat; 1426kJ (341 cal)*

---

mini lemon yogurt cakes with syrup

preparation time 10 minutes cooking time 15 minutes makes 30

The combination of lemon, yogurt and poppy seeds lends an eastern Mediterranean accent to these morsels.

⅓ cup (50g) self-raising flour

¼ cup (55g) caster sugar

1½ tablespoons cornflour

¼ teaspoon bicarbonate of soda

1 teaspoon poppy seeds

1 egg yolk

¼ cup (70g) natural yogurt

½ teaspoon finely grated lemon rind

1 teaspoon lemon juice

10g butter, melted

LEMON SYRUP

1 medium lemon (140g)

¼ cup (55g) sugar

¼ cup (60ml) water

1 Preheat oven to 180°C/160°C fan-forced.

2 Sift flour, sugar, cornflour and soda into small bowl; stir in seeds, yolk, yogurt, rind, juice and butter.

3 Drop rounded teaspoons of mixture into baby patty cases on oven tray. Bake about 10 minutes.

4 Meanwhile, make lemon syrup.

5 Drizzle or brush hot lemon syrup over hot cakes.

    LEMON SYRUP Using vegetable peeler, remove rind from lemon; shred peel finely. Juice the peeled lemon; place 2 teaspoons of the juice (reserve remainder for another use) in small saucepan with shredded rind, sugar and the water. Stir over heat, without boiling, until sugar dissolves. Boil, uncovered, without stirring, about 5 minutes or until mixture thickens slightly; transfer to small heatproof jug.

    PER CAKE *0.6g fat; 121kJ (29 cal)*

ALMOND
Blanched brown skins removed.
Slivered small pieces cut lengthways.

AUBERGINE also known as eggplant; often thought of as a vegetable but actually a fruit and belongs to the same family as the tomato, chilli and potato. Ranging in size from tiny to very large and in colour from pale green to deep purple. Can be purchased char-grilled, packed in oil, in jars.

BAGEL small ring-shaped bread roll; yeast-based but egg-less, with a dense, chewy texture and shiny crust. A true bagel is boiled in water before it's baked.

BAMBOO SHOOTS tender, pale yellow, edible first-growth of the bamboo plant; add crunch and fibre as well as a certain distinctive sweetness to a dish. Available fresh in Asian greengrocers, in season, but usually purchased canned; these must be drained and rinsed before use.

BICARBONATE OF SODA also known as baking soda; a mild alkali used as a leavening agent in baking.

BOTTLED TOMATO PASTA SAUCE a prepared tomato-based sauce (sometimes called ragu or sugo on the label); comes in varying degrees of thickness and with different flavourings.

BREADCRUMBS
Fresh bread, usually white, processed into crumbs; good for poultry stuffings and as a thickening agent in some soups and cold sauces.
Packaged prepared fine-textured but crunchy white breadcrumbs; good for coating or crumbing foods that are to be fried.
Stale crumbs made by grating, blending or processing 1- or 2-day-old bread.

BUK CHOY also known as bok choy, pak choi, chinese white cabbage or chinese chard; has a fresh, mild mustard taste. Use both stems and leaves, stir-fried or braised. Baby buk choy, also known as pak kat farang or shanghai bok choy, is much smaller and more tender than buk choy. Its mildly acrid, distinctively appealing taste has made it one of the most commonly used Asian greens.

CHEESE
Fetta Greek in origin; a crumbly textured goat- or sheep-milk cheese having a sharp, salty taste. Ripened and stored in salted whey; particularly good cubed and tossed into salads.
Mozzarella soft, spun-curd cheese; originating in southern Italy where it was traditionally made from water-buffalo milk. Now generally manufactured from cow milk, it is the most popular pizza cheese because of its low melting point and elasticity when heated (used for texture rather than flavour).
Parmesan also known as parmigiano, parmesan is a hard, grainy cow-milk cheese which originated in the Parma region of Italy. The curd for this cheese is salted in brine for a month before being aged for up to 2 years, preferably in humid conditions.
Ricotta a soft, sweet, moist, white cow-milk cheese with a low fat content (about 8.5 per cent) and a slightly grainy texture. The name roughly translates as "cooked again" and refers to ricotta's manufacture from a whey that is itself a by-product of other cheese making.

CHOCOLATE
Choc Bits also known as chocolate chips or chocolate morsels; available in milk, white and dark chocolate. Made of cocoa liquor, cocoa butter, sugar and an emulsifier, these hold their shape in baking and are ideal for decorating.
Dark eating also known as semi-sweet or luxury chocolate; made of a high percentage of cocoa liquor and cocoa butter, and little added sugar. Unless stated otherwise, we use dark eating chocolate in this book as it's ideal for use in desserts and cakes.
Hazelnut spread we used Nutella.
Milk eating most popular eating chocolate, mild and very sweet; similar in make-up to dark with the difference being the addition of milk solids.

CHORIZO sausage of Spanish origin, made of coarsely ground pork and highly seasoned with garlic and chilli.

CORIANDER also known as cilantro, pak chee or chinese parsley; bright-green-leafed herb having both pungent aroma and taste.

CORNFLOUR also known as cornstarch. Available made from corn or wheat (wheaten cornflour, gluten-free, gives a lighter texture in cakes); used as a thickening agent in cooking

COS LETTUCE also known as romaine lettuce; the traditional caesar salad lettuce. Long, with leaves ranging from dark green on the outside to almost white near the core; the leaves have a stiff centre rib that gives a slight cupping effect to the leaf on either side.

COUSCOUS a fine, grain-like cereal product made from semolina; from the countries of North Africa. A semolina flour and water dough is sieved then dehydrated to produce minuscule even-sized pellets of couscous; it is rehydrated by steaming or with the addition of a warm liquid and swells to three or four times its original size; eaten like rice with a tagine, as a side dish or in a salad.

DESIREE POTATO oval, smooth and pink-skinned, waxy yellow flesh; good in salads, boiled and roasted.

DATES fruit of the date palm tree, eaten fresh or dried, on their own or in prepared dishes. About 4cm to 6cm in length, oval and plump, thin-skinned, with a honey-sweet flavour and sticky texture.

FISH SAUCE called naam pla on the label if Thai-made, nuoc naam if Vietnamese; the two are almost identical. Made from pulverised salted fermented fish (most often anchovies); has a pungent smell and strong taste. Available in varying degrees of intensity, so use according to your taste.

GELATINE we use dried (powdered) gelatine in the recipes in this book; it's also available in sheet form known as leaf gelatine. A thickening agent made from either collagen, a protein found in animal connective tissue and bones, or certain algae (agar-agar). Three teaspoons of dried gelatine (8g or one sachet) is roughly equivalent to four gelatine leaves.

GREEN ONION also known as scallion or (incorrectly) shallot; an immature onion picked before the bulb has formed, having a long, bright-green edible stalk.

GLOSSARY

KECAP MANIS a dark, thick sweet soy sauce used in most South-East Asian cuisines. Depending on the manufacturer, the sauces's sweetness is derived from the addition of either molasses or palm sugar when brewed.

KIDNEY BEANS medium-size red bean, slightly floury in texture yet sweet in flavour; sold dried or canned, it's found in bean mixes and is the bean used in chilli con carne.

KUMARA the polynesian name of an orange-fleshed sweet potato often confused with yam; good baked, boiled, mashed or fried similarly to other potatoes.

MAPLE SYRUP distilled from the sap of sugar maple trees found only in Canada and about ten states in the USA. Most often eaten with pancakes or waffles, but also used as an ingredient in baking or in preparing desserts. Maple-flavoured syrup or pancake syrup is not an adequate substitute for the real thing.

MILK

Buttermilk in spite of its name, buttermilk is actually low in fat, varying between 0.6 per cent and 2.0 per cent per 100 ml. Originally the term given to the slightly sour liquid left after butter was churned from cream, today it is intentionally made from no-fat or low-fat milk to which specific bacterial cultures have been added during the manufacturing process.

Coconut not the liquid found inside the fruit, which is called coconut water, but the diluted liquid from the second pressing of the white flesh of a mature coconut (the first pressing produces coconut cream). Available in cans and cartons at most supermarkets.

Evaporated unsweetened canned milk from which water has been extracted by evaporation. Evaporated skim or low-fat milk has 0.3 per cent fat content.

MIRIN a Japanese champagne-coloured cooking wine, made of glutinous rice and alcohol. It is used expressly for cooking and should not be confused with sake.

OIL

Olive made from ripened olives. Extra virgin and virgin are the first and second press, respectively, of the olives and are therefore considered the best; the "extra light" or "light" name on other types refers to taste not fat levels.

Peanut pressed from ground peanuts; the most commonly used oil in Asian cooking because of its high smoke point (capacity to handle high heat without burning).

Sesame made from roasted, crushed, white sesame seeds; a flavouring rather than a cooking medium.

Vegetable any of a number of oils sourced from plant rather than animal fats.

PECAN native to the US and now grown locally; pecans are golden brown, buttery and rich. Good in savoury as well as sweet dishes; walnuts are a good substitute.

PINE NUTS also known as pignoli; not in fact a nut but a small, cream-coloured kernel from pine cones. They are best roasted before use to bring out the flavour.

POLENTA also known as cornmeal; a flour-like cereal made of dried corn (maize). Also the name of the dish made from it.

READY-ROLLED PUFF PASTRY sheets of puff pastry, available from supermarkets.

RED CURRY PASTE probably the most popular thai curry paste; a hot blend of different flavours that complements the richness of pork, duck and seafood. Also works well stirred into marinades and sauces.

RICE PAPER SHEETS there are two products sold as rice paper. Banh trang is made from rice flour and water then stamped into rounds; is quite brittle and breaks easily. Dipped briefly in water, they become pliable wrappers for food.

RICE VERMICELLI also known as sen mee, mei fun or bee hoon. Used throughout Asia in spring rolls and cold salads; similar to bean threads, only longer and made with rice flour instead of mung bean starch. Soak the dried noodles in hot water until softened, boil them briefly then rinse with hot water.

ROLLED OATS flattened oat grain rolled into flakes and traditionally used for porridge. Instant oats are also available, but use traditional oats for baking.

SNAKE BEANS long (about 40cm), thin, round, fresh green beans, Asian in origin, with a taste similar to green or french beans. Used most frequently in stir-fries, they are also known as yard-long beans because of their (pre-metric) length.

SOY SAUCE

Light fairly thin in consistency and, while paler than the others, the saltiest tasting; used in dishes in which the natural colour of the ingredients is to be maintained.

Japanese an all-purpose low-sodium soy sauce made with more wheat content than its Chinese counterparts; fermented in barrels and aged. Possibly the best table soy and the one to choose if you only want one variety.

SWEET CHILLI SAUCE comparatively mild, fairly sticky and bottled sauce made from red chillies, sugar, garlic and white vinegar; used in Thai cooking and as a condiment.

SWEET PAPRIKA ground dried sweet red bell pepper; there are many grades and types available, including sweet, hot, mild and smoked.

TAHINI sesame seed paste available from Middle Eastern food stores; most often used in hummus and baba ghanoush.

TOFU also known as soybean curd or bean curd; an off-white, custard-like product made from the "milk" of crushed soybeans. Comes fresh as soft or firm, and processed as fried or pressed dried sheets. Fresh tofu can be refrigerated in water (changed daily) for up to four days.

TURKISH BREAD also known as pide. Sold in long (about 45cm) flat loaves as well as individual rounds; made from wheat flour and sprinkled with black onion seeds.

VANILLA

Bean dried, long, thin pod from a tropical golden orchid grown in central and South America and Tahiti; the minuscule black seeds inside the bean are used to impart a luscious vanilla flavour in baking and desserts. Place a whole bean in a jar of sugar to make the vanilla sugar often called for in recipes; a bean can be used three or four times before losing its flavour.

Extract obtained from vanilla beans infused in water; a non-alcoholic version of essence.

WATER CHESTNUTS resemble true chestnuts in appearance, hence the English name. Small brown tubers with a crisp, white, nutty-tasting flesh. Their crunchy texture is best experienced fresh; however, canned water chestnuts are more easily obtained and can be kept for about a month in the fridge, once opened. Used, rinsed and drained, in salads and stir-fries.

WOMBOK also known as chinese cabbage, peking or napa cabbage; elongated in shape with pale green, crinkly leaves, this is the most common cabbage in South-East Asia, forming the basis of the pickled Korean condiment, kim chi.

WONTON WRAPPERS and gow gee or spring roll pastry sheets, made of flour, egg and water, are found in the freezer or refrigerated sections of Asian food shops and many supermarkets.

ZUCCHINI also known as courgette; small, pale- or dark-green, yellow or white vegetable belonging to the squash family.

MEASURES

One Australian metric measuring cup holds approximately 250ml; one Australian metric tablespoon holds 20ml; one Australian metric teaspoon holds 5ml.

The difference between one country's measuring cups and another's is within a two- or three-teaspoon variance, and will not affect your cooking results. North America, New Zealand and the United Kingdom use a 15ml tablespoon.

All cup and spoon measurements are level. The most accurate way of measuring dry ingredients is to weigh them. When measuring liquids, use a clear glass or plastic jug with the metric markings.

We use large eggs with an average weight of 60g.

DRY MEASURES

METRIC	IMPERIAL
15g	½oz
30g	1oz
60g	2oz
90g	3oz
125g	4oz (¼lb)
155g	5oz
185g	6oz
220g	7oz
250g	8oz (½lb)
280g	9oz
315g	10oz
345g	11oz
375g	12oz (¾lb)
410g	13oz
440g	14oz
470g	15oz
500g	16oz (1lb)
750g	24oz (1½lb)
1kg	32oz (2lb)

LIQUID MEASURES

METRIC	IMPERIAL
30ml	1 fluid oz
60ml	2 fluid oz
100ml	3 fluid oz
125ml	4 fluid oz
150ml	5 fluid oz (¼ pint/1 gill)
190ml	6 fluid oz
250ml	8 fluid oz
300ml	10 fluid oz (½ pint)
500ml	16 fluid oz
600ml	20 fluid oz (1 pint)
1000ml (1 litre)	1¾ pints

LENGTH MEASURES

METRIC	IMPERIAL
3mm	⅛in
6mm	¼in
1cm	½in
2cm	¾in
2.5cm	1in
5cm	2in
6cm	2½in
8cm	3in
10cm	4in
13cm	5in
15cm	6in
18cm	7in
20cm	8in
23cm	9in
25cm	10in
28cm	11in
30cm	12in (1ft)

OVEN TEMPERATURES

These oven temperatures are only a guide for conventional ovens.
For fan-forced ovens, check the manufacturer's manual.

	°C (CELSIUS)	°F (FAHRENHEIT)	GAS MARK
Very slow	120	250	½
Slow	150	275-300	1-2
Moderately slow	160	325	3
Moderate	180	350-375	4-5
Moderately hot	200	400	6
Hot	220	425-450	7-8
Very hot	240	475	9

CONVERSION CHART

A

apple bread and butter pudding 101
artichoke, chicken and
    lemon skewers 70
artichoke risotto 45
aubergine
    baba ghanoush 32
    roasted vegetable lasagne 42
    vegetable moussaka 41

B

baba ghanoush 32
bacon, cheese and chilli muffins 24
bagel chips 32
banana passionfruit soy smoothie 7
bean and beef tacos 89
beef
    beef and bean tacos 89
    beef and onion kebabs 85
    beef in red wine 54
    beef, red wine and chilli casserole
      with polenta 85
    crisp beef with baby
      buk choy and noodles 93
    meatballs in rosemary
      paprika sauce 86
    red beef curry 89
    satay beef with rice 90
    steak diane 82
beetroot and tzatziki,
    lamb patties with 81
beetroot dip, quick 32
berry smoothie 7
black forest parfaits 110
blueberry muffins 16
blueberry sauce, strawberry
    hotcakes with 19
bread and butter pudding, apple 101
breakfast with the lot 27
bruschetta 30
    courgette and pine nut 30
    roasted red pepper and olive 31
    tomato and basil 31
buk choy and garlic prawns
    with herbed rice 62

buttermilk ice-cream, honey, with
    fresh fruit salsa 113

C

cafe latte, vanilla 11
cantonese steamed ginger snapper 61
caramelised onion and red lentil dip 35
carrot, orange and ginger juice 6
casserole, chilli, with polenta, beef
    and red wine 85
cheesecake, lime 109
chicken
    chicken and lentil cacciatore 69
    chicken, lemon and
      artichoke skewers 70
    chorizo-stuffed roast chicken 65
    ginger chicken kebabs 69
    grilled tandoori chicken 73
    spanish chicken casserole 66
chilli casserole with polenta, beef
    and red wine 85
chilli pizza rounds 36
chocolate
    black forest parfaits 110
    brownie 106
    chocolate hazelnut croissants 28
    chocolate ricotta tart 102
    iced mocha 10
    mousse 102
    real hot chocolate 11
    spiced chocolate milk 10
chorizo-stuffed roast chicken 65
citrus compote 12
coconut mango thickshake 8
corned beef hash patties with
    poached eggs 23
courgette and pine nut bruschetta 30
couscous, lamb hot-pot with 78
cranberry syrup, pears poached in 106
croissants, chocolate hazelnut 28
curry, red beef 89

D

dips
    baba ghanoush 32
    beetroot 32

caramelised onion and red lentil 35
    spicy tomato salsa 32

E

eggs
    breakfast with the lot 27
    corned beef hash patties
      with poached eggs 23
    egg-white omelette 53
    frittata, *see frittata*

F

fetta and black olive mash 97
fish
    cantonese steamed
      ginger snapper 61
    fish kebabs with chilli sauce 94
    oven-steamed ocean trout 61
    salmon and herb soufflés 54
    salmon patties with baby spinach 57
    salmon rice paper rolls 57
fresh fruit salsa, honey buttermilk
    ice-cream with 113
frittata
    leek, spinach and mushroom 50
    mini spinach 20
    silverbeet, mushroom and
      red pepper 49

G

garlic prawns and buk choy
    with herbed rice 62
ginger, carrot and orange juice 6
ginger chicken kebabs 69

H

ham, roast garlic mushrooms
    with crispy 20
honey buttermilk ice-cream
    with fresh fruit salsa 113

I

ice-cream, honey buttermilk, with
    fresh fruit salsa 113

ARE YOU MISSING SOME OF THE WORLD'S FAVOURITE COOKBOOKS?

The Australian Women's Weekly Cookbooks are available from bookshops, cookshops, supermarkets and other stores all over the world. You can also buy direct from the publisher, using the order form below.

ACP Magazines Ltd Privacy Notice
This book may contain offers, competitions or surveys that require you to provide information about yourself if you choose to enter or take part in any such Reader Offer. If you provide information about yourself to ACP Magazines Ltd, the company will use this information to provide you with the products or services you have requested, and may supply your information to contractors that help ACP to do this. ACP will also use your information to inform you of other ACP publications, products, services and events. ACP will also give your information to organisations that are providing special prizes or offers, and that are clearly associated with the Reader Offer. Unless you tell us not to, we may give your information to other organisations that use it to inform you about other products, services and events or who may give it to other organisations that may use it for this purpose. If you would like to gain access to the information ACP holds about you, please contact ACP's Privacy Officer at ACP Magazines Ltd, 54-58 Park Street, Sydney, NSW 2000, Australia.

☐ **Privacy Notice** Please do not provide information about me to any organisation not associated with this offer.

To order: Mail or fax – photocopy or complete the order form above, and send your credit card details or cheque payable to: Australian Consolidated Press (UK), ACP Books, 10 Scirocco Close, Moulton Park Office Village, Northampton NN3 6AP
phone (+44) (0)1604 642 200
fax (+44) (0)1604 642 300
email books@acpuk.com
or order online at www.acpuk.com
Non-UK residents: We accept the credit cards listed on the coupon, or cheques, drafts or International Money Orders payable in sterling and drawn on a UK bank. Credit card charges are at the exchange rate current at the time of payment.
Postage and packing UK: Add £1.00 per order plus £1.75 per book.
Postage and packing overseas: Add £2.00 per order plus £3.50 per book.
All pricing current at time of going to press and subject to change/availability.
Offer ends 31.12.2008

TITLE	RRP	QTY	TITLE	RRP	QTY
100 Fast Fillets	£6.99		Indian Cooking Class	£6.99	
After Work Fast	£6.99		Japanese Cooking Class	£6.99	
Beginners Cooking Class	£6.99		Just For One	£6.99	
Beginners Thai	£6.99		Just For Two	£6.99	
Best Food Desserts	£6.99		Kids' Birthday Cakes	£6.99	
Best Food Fast	£6.99		Kids Cooking	£6.99	
Breads & Muffins	£6.99		Kids' Cooking Step-by-Step	£6.99	
Cafe Classics	£6.99		Low-carb, Low-fat	£6.99	
Cakes, Bakes & Desserts	£6.99		Low-fat Feasts	£6.99	
Cakes Biscuits & Slices	£6.99		Low-fat Food for Life	£6.99	
Cakes Cooking Class	£6.99		Low-fat Meals in Minutes	£6.99	
Caribbean Cooking	£6.99		Main Course Salads	£6.99	
Casseroles	£6.99		Mexican	£6.99	
Casseroles & Slow-Cooked Classics	£6.99		Middle Eastern Cooking Class	£6.99	
Cheap Eats	£6.99		Mince in Minutes	£6.99	
Cheesecakes: baked and chilled	£6.99		Moroccan & the Foods of North Africa	£6.99	
Chicken	£6.99		Muffins, Scones & Breads	£6.99	
Chicken Meals in Minutes	£6.99		New Casseroles	£6.99	
Chinese & the foods of Thailand, Vietnam, Malaysia & Japan	£6.99		New Curries	£6.99	
			New Finger Food	£6.99	
Chinese Cooking Class	£6.99		New French Food	£6.99	
Christmas Cooking	£6.99		New Salads	£6.99	
Chocolate	£6.99		Party Food and Drink	£6.99	
Chocs & Treats	£6.99		Pasta Meals in Minutes	£6.99	
Cocktails	£6.99		Potatoes	£6.99	
Cookies & Biscuits	£6.99		Rice & Risotto	£6.99	
Cupcakes & Fairycakes	£6.99		Salads: Simple, Fast & Fresh	£6.99	
Detox	£6.99		Sauces Salsas & Dressings	£6.99	
Dinner Lamb	£6.99		Sensational Stir-Fries	£6.99	
Dinner Seafood	£6.99		Simple Healthy Meals	£6.99	
Easy Curry	£6.99		Soup	£6.99	
Easy Midweek Meals	£6.99		Stir-fry	£6.99	
Easy Spanish-Style	£6.99		Superfoods for Exam Success	£6.99	
Essential Soup	£6.99		Sweet Old-Fashioned Favourites	£6.99	
Food for Fit and Healthy Kids	£6.99		Tapas Mezze Antipasto & other bites	£6.99	
Foods of the Mediterranean	£6.99		Thai Cooking Class	£6.99	
Foods That Fight Back	£6.99		Traditional Italian	£6.99	
Fresh Food Fast	£6.99		Vegetarian Meals in Minutes	£6.99	
Fresh Food for Babies & Toddlers	£6.99		Vegie Food	£6.99	
Good Food for Babies & Toddlers	£6.99		Wicked Sweet Indulgences	£6.99	
Greek Cooking Class	£6.99		Wok, Meals in Minutes	£6.99	
Grills	£6.99				
Healthy Heart Cookbook	£6.99		TOTAL COST:	£	

Mr/Mrs/Ms _____

Address _____

_____ Postcode _____

Day time phone _____ Email* (optional) _____

I enclose my cheque/money order for £ _____

or please charge £ _____

to my: ☐ Access   ☐ Mastercard   ☐ Visa   ☐ Diners Club

Card number ☐☐☐☐ ☐☐☐☐ ☐☐☐☐ ☐☐☐☐

Expiry date _____ 3 digit security code *(found on reverse of card)* _____

Cardholder's name_____ Signature _____

* By including your email address, you consent to receipt of any email regarding this magazine, and other emails which inform you of ACP's other publications, products, services and events, and to promote third party goods and services you may be interested in.

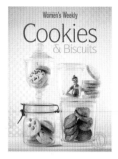
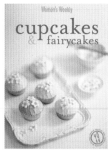
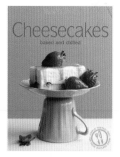

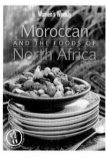

You'll find these books and more available on sale at bookshops, cookshops, selected supermarkets or direct from the publisher (see order form page 119).

TEST KITCHEN

Food director Pamela Clark

Test Kitchen manager Kellie-Marie Thomas

Nutritional information Belinda Farlow

ACP BOOKS

Editorial director Susan Tomnay

Creative director Hieu Chi Nguyen

Designer Caryl Wiggins

Director of sales Brian Cearnes

Marketing manager Bridget Cody

Business analyst Ashley Davies

Production manager Cedric Taylor

Chief executive officer Ian Law

Group publisher Pat Ingram

General manager Christine Whiston

Editorial director (WW) Deborah Thomas

RIGHTS ENQUIRIES

Laura Bamford, Director ACP Books

lbamford@acpuk.com

Produced by ACP Books, Sydney.

Printed by Dai Nippon, c/o Samhwa Printing Co., Ltd, 237-10 Kuro-Dong, Kuro-Ku, Seoul, Korea.

Published by ACP Books, a division of ACP Magazines Ltd, 54 Park St, Sydney; GPO Box 4088, Sydney, NSW 2001.

Ph: (02) 9282 8618 Fax: (02) 9267 9438.

acpbooks@acpmagazines.com.au

www.acpbooks.com.au

To order books, phone 136 116 (within Australia).

Send recipe enquiries to:

recipeenquiries@acpmagazines.com.au

Australia Distributed by Network Services, phone +61 2 9282 8777 fax +61 2 9264 3278 networkweb@networkservicescompany.com.au

United Kingdom Distributed by Australian Consolidated Press (UK), phone (01604) 642 200 fax (01604) 642 300 books@acpuk.com

New Zealand Distributed by Netlink Distribution Company, phone (9) 366 9966 ask@ndc.co.nz

South Africa Distributed by PSD Promotions, phone (27 11) 392 6065/7 fax (27 11) 392 6079/80 orders@psdprom.co.za

Simple healthy meals: the Australian women's weekly.

Includes index.

ISBN 978 186396 720 4 (pbk.).

1. Quick and easy cookery. I. Clark, Pamela.

II. Title: Australian women's weekly.

641.5

© ACP Magazines Ltd 2007

ABN 18 053 273 546